WHEN
TEACHERS
PRAY

WHEN TEACHERS PRAY

THE POWER *of a*
PERSONAL PRAYER LIFE

VICKI CARUANA

America's Teacher™ *and author of*
APPLES AND CHALKDUST

BROADMAN
&HOLMAN
PUBLISHERS

NASHVILLE, TENNESSEE

© 2004 by Vicki Caruana
All rights reserved
Printed in the United States of America

0-8054-3095-4

Published by Broadman & Holman Publishers,
Nashville, Tennessee

Dewey Decimal Classification: 371.1
Subject Heading: TEACHERS \ PRAYER

All Scripture quotations, unless otherwise indicated,
are taken from the Holman Christian Standard Bible,
© 1999, 2000, 2001, and 2003.

1 2 3 4 5 6 7 8 9 10 08 07 06 05 04

Dedication

To my mother, whose constant prayers I know sustain me.

Acknowledgments

To Jennifer Kennedy Dean, whose friendship teaches me
new things about prayer every time we speak.
To Ellie Kay, who I can count on to pray God's Word back to me
even in the most discouraging of situations.
To Denise Winchell, whose thorough knowledge of the Word of
God keeps me focused and grounded in what is true.

Contents

Foreword   ix

Introduction   1
How to Use This Book   3

Chapter 1: The Power of a Praying Teacher   5
Chapter 2: Lord, Teach Us to Pray   14
Chapter 3: Pray the Issues: Student Behavior   25
Chapter 4: Pray the Issues: Relationships with Parents   35
Chapter 5: Pray the Issues: Relationships with Other Teachers and Staff   44
Chapter 6: Pray the Issues: Submitting to Authority   52
Chapter 7: Pray the Issues: Disappointment   62
Chapter 8: Pray the Issues: Discouragement   73
Chapter 9: Pray the Issues: Danger   85
Chapter 10: Pray the Issues: Lack of Respect   96
Chapter 11: Pray the Issues: Lack of Funds   107
Chapter 12: Prayer in Schools and out of Schools   116

Resources   131
Notes   133

Foreword

Vicki Caruana has put her finger on God's pulse. She has found his heartbeat. Prayer! The key to Kingdom treasure is earnest, persevering prayer.

Imagine a school seeded with teachers who understand and embrace the power of prayer. Imagine the halls and classrooms of that school echoing with the prayers of teachers—an echo not heard by human ears but one that reverberates in the heavens. "Let your Kingdom come in this place. Let your will be done in this place." Can you imagine it?

My friend, you *cannot* imagine it. Think your highest thought, and God's will be higher. Make your grandest plan, and God's will top it. Dream your biggest dream, and God's will overwhelm it. He is able to do *more*. "Now to Him who is able to do above and beyond all that we ask or think—according to the power that works in you" (Eph. 3:20). We cannot even think of all that God would do through his strategically positioned teachers who know how to pray with power.

Vicki brings the eternal principles of prayer into the daily experiences of teachers. She is uniquely qualified to write such a book as this because she knows both the heart of God and the hearts of teachers. Teacher that she is, she proclaims the truths about prayer clearly and makes the school environment a prayer lab—a place to put truth into practice and observe its results.

She gently leads teachers to a deeper intimacy with the Father as she encourages them to use their daily challenges and struggles to let him work in their own lives. She understands the primary truth about praying with power: it flows from a life that is filled with Christ. "On the last and most important day of the festival, Jesus stood up and cried out, 'If anyone is thirsty, he should come to Me and drink! The one who believes in Me, as the Scripture has said, will have streams of living water flow from deep within him'" (John 7:37–38). Imagine. The power of God flowing like a river, changing the landscape in its wake.

Teachers, let Vicki lead you to the great discovery: God's power is at work in and through you. How is it that he will do immeasurably more than we ask or think? "according to *the power* that works *in you*" (Eph. 3:20 [emphasis added]). Prayer releases the power of God to accomplish the purposes of God. Let the River flow!

Jennifer Kennedy Dean
Executive Director, The Praying Life Foundation
Author, *Legacy of Prayer: A Spiritual Trust Fund for the Generations*

Introduction

When I taught in the public schools, it was always a pleasant surprise for me to discover other Christian teachers in my midst. Somehow God always revealed them to me, and I was grateful. But even that knowledge doesn't break the isolation many teachers feel on a daily basis. We still feel like lonely soldiers, barely holding the line, wondering if anyone will come alongside to hold it with us. Our conversations in the teachers' lounge aren't always Christlike. Our reactions to inequities and injustices don't always lead anyone else to believe we belong to Almighty God. We look, speak, and act the same as everyone else in our school.

Even as I run into teachers now at a social gathering or a conference of some kind, the conversations inevitably turn out the same. They are full of disappointment, disillusionment, and even despair. I look into their eyes and see broken hearts. I listen to their voices and hear indescribable pain. We walk around believing we can do nothing to change our situations, forgetting the power that is already within us—forgetting the only salve that can soothe our raw spirits. The Word of God is the only thing that is powerful enough to overcome any and all of our troubles. Coupled with the prayers of other believing teachers, our cries are heard, and our spirits can be lifted.

We spend a great deal of time learning about our craft in order to be better teachers. We spend a great deal of energy making ourselves look better on the outside. Yet our spirits are dying inside. Is it that we discount the power of prayer, or do we even consider it at all? We know that more money, new programs, or even national certification can't heal what ails us. Stop trying to fix it all by yourself and submit to the power of the God of the universe, whose unfailing love changes everything! Join together with your brothers and sisters in Christ in your schools and create a prayed-for school. And then watch what God does!

Vicki Caruana is the founder of Teachers in Prayer, a group that sponsors teacher prayer conferences around the country. Find out how you can encourage other teachers or schedule a speaking engagement in your area by visiting her Web site at www.apples andchalkdust.com.

How to Use This Book

When Teachers Pray is ideal for either individual or group study. At the end of each chapter you will find three study components: prayer points, prayer prompts, and a sample prayer. "Prayer Points" direct you to verses that complement the topic that chapter presents. Use them as a starting point, but you can encourage members of your group to seek other verses that apply the same chapter concept. "Prayer Prompts" can be used for meditation, discussion, or journaling. They ask you to apply what you've learned in a chapter to your real life in the classroom. These prompts can bring together members of a newly formed prayer group. A sample prayer concludes each chapter. You may pray this aloud in your group or silently. Or use it merely as a starting point for your own prayer time with the Lord.

The themes in *When Teachers Pray* are universal for all teachers, yet individual circumstances may vary. Apply the concepts you learn to your own situation. If used as a group study, one chapter per week is the recommended course of study. Allow an hour for each study session. That gives individual teachers time to share their burdens and then actively pray for one another.

Chapter 1

CRY OUT TO THE LORD!

The Power of a Praying Teacher

*[Jesus] then told them a parable on the need for them
to pray always and not become discouraged:
"There was a judge in one town who didn't fear God or respect
man. And a widow in that town kept coming to him, saying,
'Give me justice against my adversary.'
For a while he was unwilling, but later he said to himself,
'Even though I don't fear God or respect man, yet because
this widow keeps pestering me, I will give her justice, so she
doesn't wear me out by her persistent coming.'"
Then the Lord said, "Listen to what the unjust judge says.
Will not God grant justice to His elect who cry out to Him
day and night? Will He delay [to help] them? I tell you that
He will swiftly grant them justice. Nevertheless, when the
Son of Man comes, will He find that faith on earth?"*

LUKE 18:1–8

Surveying your class roster can be a discouraging task. Another teacher is bound to look over your shoulder and sigh at your prospects. Even before the first day of school, you know who is in special education, who has a high-maintenance parent, and who has been a troublemaker in the past. It makes it quite difficult to walk in that first day with much optimism.

We have been given a vast variety of strategies and techniques to use with difficult students and parents. We are also encouraged to solve any problems we encounter on our own. Asking for help may be seen as a sign of weakness, and the consequence of an unrenewed contract looms. Yet the problems remain and even grow to unmanageable proportions. Where do you turn?

God encourages us to cry out to him. When we cry out, we show that we know he is there and that he is the only one who can do what we ask. Unlike our earthly authorities, crying out for help is seen as strong faith and not weak work in the eyes of our God. Bring your roster of student names before him daily. Pray over and over again about the boy who is constantly testing you, the girl who seems friendless, or the parent who calls your home after 10 P.M. on a regular basis. Prayer is your most effective strategy. It is the one thing that works for all people in every situation.

A praying teacher is a productive teacher. Prayer is not a passive behavior—it is instead an active pursuit. Prayer is not a last-ditch effort—it is instead your most powerful offensive weapon. The Holy Spirit prompts us to pray and invites us to be a part of the process of making God's will as it is in heaven here on earth. It is a continuous dialogue between Father and child. It is our only reliable means of educational reform. Prayer doesn't just change the lives of those we pray for—it forever changes the life of the pray-er.

As It Is in Heaven

Sometimes when we pray, our prayer turns into a list as long as our students' school supply list. The irony is that we tend to pray for what we "want" not necessarily for what we "need." Likewise, that school supply list often is really a list of wants. After all, children are supposed to receive a *free* public education. Those lists are, in reality, extras, but they've been used for so long that we've forgotten they are just *wants*. When we pray, we may be so used to rattling off a list to God that we forget he will provide for our needs. Sometimes we don't even know what to pray for. The situation may be so messy that it's all we can do to surrender and cry out to God for help.

When we do cry out to him, what does that cry imply? It says, "Do something, God!" "Take over, Lord. Do it your way!" or "My way's not working, Lord. I give up!" It usually isn't until we come to the end of ourselves that we cry out to God for his will to be done in a particular situation. Instead of waiting until we are at our wit's end, we need to cultivate a persistent dialogue with God. That way, in each and every circumstance we can say with confidence, "Let your will be done in this situation, Lord." When we reach that level of intimacy with God, we will project a peaceful, contented attitude to all those around us. Teachers who still struggle with wanting their own will to be done will wonder how a person can be at peace in the midst of the storm.

As teachers we are accustomed to being the expert. So many people come to us for answers. Students come to us. Parents come to us. Friends and family come to us when they have a "school" question. It's not easy to give up that expert status when we pray. We think we know the right solution and pray that God will bless it. But it doesn't work that way. Part of the problem is that we are more concerned with our own reputations. We worry about what parents think of us. We worry about what our colleagues and principals think of us. We worry that the students won't like us. Our glory is not what matters. What does matter is whether what we do, what we say, and how we say it brings glory to God. That is his will for us. We were made for that perfect purpose. His will is all that matters. If you've been clinging tightly to your expert standing, now is the time to let go and hand over the reigns to the only one whose reputation matters.

Teacher/God Conferences

Our experiences with parent/teacher conferences, our conversations with those in authority over us, and our efforts to communicate knowledge to students all play a part in what we think about prayer. In all of these scenarios we are on our guard, often not trusting the motives of those with whom we are involved. We are told to document any and all conversations to protect ourselves and the school. Getting to know someone is difficult when both of you have a protective wall up for self-preservation. So instead we keep everything that causes us anguish tucked inside, safe from those who might exploit it as weakness. We find ourselves utterly alone.

Yet all is not lost. We are not alone. The omnipresent God assures us of that. He is there in the middle of the muck. He is there when you are being belittled by your principal. He is there when you are confronted by a belligerent parent. He is there when you are threatened by a student. You can conference with him at a moment's notice in the midst of the mire of this place we call school. You don't need an appointment. You don't need to censor your emotions for him. You don't have to document the conversation (unless of course you journal!). He's just waiting for you to realize that the connection is open and always has been. He's waiting just for you!

We can enter into God's very presence the moment our hearts

open in silent prayer. Prayer ushers us into God's inner sanctum, what Theresa of Avila called the interior castle. The Jewish believers called it the Holy of Holies—the inner sanctuary. Only a high priest could enter into the inner sanctuary. And that high priest had to be properly prepared to enter into God's presence or face certain death. But now that Jesus Christ has come and bridged the gap between man and God, we are not only welcome in the Holy of Holies, but we are properly prepared by God's own Son. The death and resurrection of Christ prepared the way. You are welcome because it is your home—you are not a visitor but a son or daughter of the King. You belong!

As a teacher you must keep a certain distance from your students in order to be effective. If you get too close, it may compromise your judgment. After all, you are their teacher not their friend. So, too, must you maintain a professional distance from your colleagues and administrators. If those lines are blurred, their authority over you is then compromised. What a dilemma for a teacher who longs to be in relationship with those she chooses to serve! Education is about relationship, but there are boundaries. Aren't you glad that your Heavenly Father has no such boundaries? The lines were meant to be blurred! You can come to him as you are. If you are brokenhearted, bring him your broken heart in prayer. If you are wrongly accused, bring him your tarnished name in prayer. There is nothing about your situation that he cannot handle. After all, he created all things, and all things are in subjection to him. There is nothing too big for God.

REFORM OR RENEWAL?

Educational reform is the cross fire in which we, as teachers, find ourselves. Should we pray for reform? First, it's important to understand what reform means before we pray for it. It may not be what education really needs. Maybe what education and educators really need is renewal.

By definition, *reform* means "to change from worse to better"—more specifically, "to make right again." Public education, however, did not start out in a perfect or "right" state to which it can now return. There have been many stages in American education, all of which were flawed for one group of children or another. Every reform effort that has been proposed takes us back to one or another already-tried, already-impaired past. Any teacher in the classroom for more than twenty years will tell you that. That's why it's so hard to get excited about any of the proposed reforms.

We are expected to submit to those in authority, whether they are district superintendents, state governors, or federal lawmakers and whether or not we agree with their reforms. Teachers have make-it-or-break-it power when it comes to changes or new ideas in education. I know this may unsettle you, but we should not have such power. What we can do is the best job we can to the glory of God and pray that his will is done in every situation we encounter during times of great strife or uncertainty. In doing this we allow the Holy Spirit to renew us from the inside out and unleash his power into not only our lives but the lives of the students we teach.

Therefore renewal is what we seek, not reform. According to *Vine's Expository Dictionary of New Testament Words*, *renewal* is defined as an "adjustment of the moral and spiritual vision and thinking to the mind of God, which is designed to have a transforming effect upon life."[1] As Christian teachers we require daily renewal in order to give our students what they need. We've been given this talent of teaching not for ourselves but for the common good. So when we pray, we first thank God for this gift he has given us. Then we pray that his Spirit will continue to renew our minds so that we will be able to say honestly, "Your will be done today in this circumstance, Lord!"

Do not be conformed to this age, but be transformed by the renewing of your mind, so that you may discern what is the good, pleasing, and perfect will of God.

ROMANS 12:2

LIFE-CHANGING POWER

People usually become teachers for two reasons: they love children, and they want to impact lives. We go into teaching believing we have all the tools to make that impact and to really change lives and mold futures. But it's not our toolbox full of teaching strategies that has this life-changing power. It's the love we have for students that makes the difference. It's the relationship we take the risk to nurture. In reality, it's God's love for us poured out into the lives of those in our charge.

I recently heard from a former student whom I taught in a college teacher education program. His greatest desire was to become a teacher and shape the future. But he struggled academically due to his own learning disabilities. Years later he found me and e-mailed me just to let me know that he did not become a teacher but entered a computer-related field instead. I was saddened by this turn of events and told him so. His response encouraged me: "You were the only teacher who really cared, Mrs. Caruana. I knew you struggled right along with me, and that meant so much." We have the opportunity each and every day to be Christ in the life of a child in our classroom. We can pray for our students to know God. We can pray for their protection. We can pray that they will use their gifts and abilities to serve God and minister to his kingdom. We can pray that we, as their teachers, will teach them only what is good, what is right, and what is pleasing in the sight of God. We can do that when we teach math. We can do that when we teach reading. We can do that when we settle disputes on the playground. We can do that when we have conferences with their parents.

Keep your eyes firmly focused on your relationship with God, and he will nurture your relationship with your students and their parents. Teachers are some of the strongest role models in a child's life, second only to their own parents. If you have a life that's been changed, let your students see it. They will follow where you lead. Just make sure it is God who lights the way.

PRAYER POINTS

- *Exodus 22:23:* "'If you do mistreat them, they will no doubt cry to Me, and I will certainly hear their cry.'"
- *Psalm 34:17:*
     "The righteous cry out, and the LORD hears,
     and delivers them from all their troubles."
- *Joel 1:14:*
     "Announce a sacred fast;
     proclaim an assembly!
     Gather the elders
     and all the residents of the land
     at the house of the LORD your God,
     and cry out to the LORD."

PRAYER PROMPT

Who will you cry out to the Lord about today? Pray for them now.

PRAY

Lord, a child is hurting. And I'm sure she's not the only one. Sometimes the children's needs seem so many and so burdensome. I feel overwhelmed by their broken spirits. How can I possibly meet all their needs and heal their broken hearts? I feel inadequate and weak. But I know you've put these particular children in my life at this time. I know that Christ's power rests on me in my weakness. So now I can delight in my weakness, for when I am weak, then I am strong. Let your glory be displayed as I console those who need consolation. Pour your mercy onto your children. Let them feel the presence of your Spirit when they come to me for help. Amen.

Chapter 2

Lord, Teach Us to Pray

Now faith is the reality of what is hoped for,
the proof of what is not seen.
HEBREWS 11:1

Whether you teach in a public school or a private Christian school, you may find that you don't pray as much as you could. As mentioned earlier, we are considered the experts, and as experts it's difficult to admit we don't have all the answers. When I switched from teaching learning disabled sixth graders to gifted sixth graders, I struggled with my expert status. Most of my gifted students knew so much more than I did. It was a challenge to stay one step ahead of them—sometimes that wasn't even possible. Our training as teachers can be an obstacle to prayer.

Another real obstacle to prayer is our territorial nature as teachers. *This is my classroom. These are my kids.* How often do you think or make those statements? We don't handle constructive criticism very well, and we rarely, if ever, ask for help. Isn't it ironic? We encourage our students to ask for help, and we provide them with constructive criticism daily. Yet we struggle with both issues ourselves. That is a hindrance to our prayer life.

Both obstacles have the same root—pride. Until we can instead practice humility, we will be solely dependent on our own abilities to solve the problems in our classrooms and schools. I'm not saying that the strategies you employ won't work otherwise, but faith in the Creator of all things will enable you to use these strategies effectively. If we want to reach the hearts of children, we can only do that with the help of the Holy Spirit. Sometimes we don't know what to do or how to pray about a given situation. The Holy Spirit does!

In the same way the Spirit also joins to help in our weakness,
because we do not know what to pray for as we should,
but the Spirit Himself intercedes for us with unspoken groanings.
And He who searches the hearts knows the Spirit's mind-set,
because He intercedes for the saints according to the will of God.
ROMANS 8:26–27

Good teachers are always learning. We've spent a lot of time and effort learning about better ways to reach our students, better ways to organize our classrooms, and better ways to manage student behavior. How much do you know about prayer? For some of us, all we know are the rote prayers of our youth. There is so much more! How then should we pray? For what should we pray?

PRAY ABOUT EVERYTHING

Don't worry about anything, but in everything, through prayer and
petition with thanksgiving, let your requests be made known to God.
PHILIPPIANS 4:6

In her book *Heart's Cry,* Jennifer Kennedy Dean says, "God wants you to let your needs and desires be known to him. He tells you not to have anxiety about anything, but instead to pray about everything. The secret, he says, is to bring your requests to him with thanksgiving."[1] Philippians 4:6 doesn't say "pray only for those things you can't handle." It doesn't say "pray when things don't work out the way you planned." It says to pray about everything. If you believe God, then you know he means exactly what he says.

As we consider what *everything* is in daily life as a teacher, we realize how frighteningly long a list it is. You could try to make such a list, but there's a good chance you'll forget something or someone. Instead allow the Holy Spirit to bring to mind those things about which you should pray. Those things that tend to cause anxiety may be more obvious to you, but what about the more subtle issues? Did you notice when you opened the car door for a student you didn't even know that her mother was distracted or maybe in more of a hurry than usual? Pray for that child. Pray for her mother. You might not know enough to pray specifically, but lift them both up to the Lord anyway. God put them in your path that day so that you could pray for them.

Once you become aware of what *everything* means, you'll be watching for prayer opportunities. You'll look at those around you differently. You'll listen more intently. You'll notice things you never noticed before. Praying for everything will become as natural as breathing.

DEVOTE YOURSELF TO PRAYER

Devote yourselves to prayer, stay alert in it with thanksgiving.
COLOSSIANS 4:2

The New King James Version says "continue earnestly in prayer." Both versions indicate that we should persevere in prayer even when we grow weary of it. Devoting yourself to someone or something means being committed unconditionally. It is an active pursuit. It is intentional. Often you don't see any changes in a colleague who treats you poorly or a student who is still failing no matter what you do. Yet we're told to continue to pray with determination. Continue to pray because the truth is that God is still there, always listening, always answering. Continue to pray because the person you are praying for benefits even if it has not been revealed to you. We don't always get to see the results of our prayers. When we do, God grants us a glimpse into his own workings, but he doesn't have to.

The second part of this verse tells us we must be *watchful and thankful* when we pray. What are we watching for? We are watching for God's answer because we know that he does indeed answer our prayers. It is an expectancy based on the truth. And the truth is that God answers prayer. We are also told to be thankful when we pray. Thanksgiving is a common component to effectual prayer. For what should we be thankful? We are thankful that the Spirit has brought this person to our mind in order that we might pray for him. We know that God's sovereign will is done on earth as it is in heaven. We pray that the commands of Scripture will be followed. We pray that we will make decisions based on what God has already taught us in his Word is righteous. We need to pray this way because even as Christians, secure in our salvation, we will falter and stumble through this life. We are thankful for God's answer, even if it comes slowly or even if it wasn't in a way that we had hoped for. Our ways are not always God's, and so we are thankful that his way prevails.

PRAY CONTINUALLY

Pray constantly.
1 THESSALONIANS 5:17

This may sound like an impossibility to us. The thought of trying to fit prayer into our already crowded day may overwhelm us, but to pray without ceasing—how is that possible? This is not a requirement to fulfill but instead a natural outcome of knowing that God is always with us. It is more an attitude that acknowledges our dependence on God. We cannot spend all our time on our knees, but it is possible to have a prayerful attitude at all times. When we realize God's constant presence within us, we will find it easier to pray frequent, spontaneous, and short prayers. A prayerful attitude is not a substitute for regular quiet times of prayer but should be an outgrowth of those times.

This is what makes prayer *in* schools possible. We don't have to formally drop to our knees, open our Bible, and pray so that all can hear. In fact, we are instructed to pray in secret instead (Matt. 6:6). We don't pray so others will hear us. Public prayer gets attention and is a self-righteous act. The essence of prayer is private communication with God. There is a place for public prayer, but to pray only where others will notice us indicates that our real audience is not God. You can have private communication with God at school. Just pray silent, short prayers right to the ear of your Heavenly Father. He's always listening.

When you feel your patience diminishing and your temper flaring, stop and pray. It is much more powerful than counting to ten or taking a time-out. Pray! Right before you make that parent phone call, pray. Pray as you go to your after-school committee meeting. Pray for children's safety at the end of the school day as they board the buses. Pray while students take the test you gave them. Pray before the day even begins that everything you say and do will please God. Continual prayer is not as demanding as it seems. It is the most important thing you will do all day.

Pray with Confession

Therefore, confess your sins to one another and pray
for one another, so that you may be healed.
The intense prayer of the righteous is very powerful.

JAMES 5:16

We know we can go directly to God for forgiveness, but confessing our sins to each other still has an important place in the life of the church. Ask God to reveal to you someone in your school whom you can trust—someone who believes just as you do. We all need someone to whom we can be accountable. That way if we sin, in word or deed, against another teacher, a parent, or even a student, we can confess that sin to a fellow believer and hear him or her assure us of God's pardon.

You can also pray for someone who has confessed to you. In doing so, his or her spirit will be soothed. Is there someone at your school who particularly annoys you? Does that person know just the right buttons to push to get you angry? Such a person may or may not confess their sin to you, but be careful you do not sin because of it. It is easy to return sin for sin. Then it is you who needs to confess. Confess your sin to another trusted believer. Then experience the healing that comes with forgiveness. If you remain in sin, God will not hear your prayers (Isa. 59:2). How then will you be able to pray for the needs of your students?

Pray with Forgiveness

And whenever you stand praying, if you have anything
against anyone, forgive him, so that your Father in heaven
will also forgive you your wrongdoing.

MARK 11:25

One of the things that hinders our prayers is failing to forgive someone else. When our prayers become complaints about a student, a parent, another teacher, or a principal, there's a good chance we've been hurt or angered by them. Often our complaints are justified, but we should not remain in a state of grievance; instead, we should pray for those who persecute us (Matt. 5:44). When the one who has wronged us is another believer, we are called to "[accept] one another and [forgive] one another if anyone has a complaint against another. Just as the Lord has forgiven you, so also you must [forgive]" (Col. 3:13).

When our prayers become prayers of forgiveness, we overcome evil with good (Rom. 12:21). We are called to forgive others, and God will then forgive us when we sin. Even when someone chronically hurts us, we must forgive. What if your team leader routinely says something to offend you, yet she asks your forgiveness each time? How many times do you forgive her? God says to forgive as many times as you are offended (Matt. 18:21–22). If you stay focused on how many times your Heavenly Father has forgiven you, it is much easier to forgive a brother or sister in the Lord. Other people around you will not understand how you could continue to forgive—but they will notice. Let them ask you how you have the capacity to forgive; it may open the door to a much deeper conversation.

PRAY WITH CONFIDENCE

Therefore let us approach the throne of grace with boldness, so that we may receive mercy and find grace to help us at the proper time.
HEBREWS 4:16

When we pray, we approach God's throne. We enter into his inner sanctuary. Only those who believe in Jesus can approach God with such confidence. We can bring him every burden, every trial, every hurt. Nothing is too little or too big to bring to the throne of heaven. God cares about the very details of our lives. He hears our prayers, extends us mercy when we fail, grants us grace when we don't deserve it, and helps us in our times of need.

Your talent of teaching is God-given. You didn't acquire it on your own. It is not a result of a college education. The confidence you have is not in yourself but in the one who created you—the Gift Giver. Confidence in Christ and arrogance are two different things. One is what we have in Christ. The other is the result of being out of fellowship with God. "These people are discontented grumblers, walking according to their desires; their mouths utter arrogant words, flattering people for their own advantage" (Jude 1:16). The teacher's lounge may be full of grumblers, faultfinders, and those who flatter others for their own advantage. Even Christian teachers struggle with these sins. Those who don't believe have no confidence to approach the throne of grace. They are not covered with the blood of Jesus in order that they may do so. As you grasp the truth of your own confidence in Christ, pray for those who do not yet know him. Pray that they, too, may be covered with the blood and enter into the inner sanctuary with boldness.

PRAY WITH OTHERS

"Again, I assure you: If two of you on earth agree about any matter that you pray for, it will be done for you by My Father in heaven. For where two or three are gathered together in My name, I am there among them."
MATTHEW 18:19–20

One day while I was substituting at my children's school, I walked into the teacher workroom to make some copies. There was a small utility closet off to one corner of the room, and the door was slightly ajar. I heard hushed voices coming from within. Normally I would have ignored them and gone about my work, but I thought what I heard was singing. I listened at the door and heard a hymn of praise being softly sung by eight teachers. I knew it was safe to invade, so I meekly asked if I could join them. This small group of teachers (in a public school) had just finished their daily prayer meeting. Even though I wasn't on staff at this school, God revealed to me a group of other believers with whom I could pray.

Because the Holy Spirit lives inside each of us as believers, we recognize one another, and the Spirit within us draws us to each other. Because we agree, the Spirit is in our midst, and we pray according to God's will. Even though we are from different backgrounds and have different needs, our prayers will blend together in one voice. It is music to God's ears.

Pray that God will reveal to you one person at school with whom you can pray. You can then pray together at a regular place and time or between classes when it's necessary. Thank God for showing you that you are not alone in your school. God cannot be kicked out of the public schools, no matter what popular culture says. He is there in each and every one of us who believe.

We are caught in the midst of a great battle—the battle for the hearts and minds of children. Sometimes the battle gets quite fierce. Sometimes we do things we wouldn't do otherwise "for the sake of the children" when in actuality we do them for our own sakes. And when the battle isn't going well and we are weary and wounded, we finally cry out to God to save us.

You do not have because you do not ask.
You ask and don't receive because you ask wrongly,
so that you may spend it on your desires for pleasure.
JAMES 4:2b–3

22

We often use prayer at the wrong time and for the wrong reasons. Instead of using prayer to call in the cavalry or reinforcements, we must see it for what it truly is—our first line of defense as well as our most effective offensive weapon. Consider what it means to put on the full armor of God. If we are going to battle, we should be prepared.

Put on the full armor of God so that you can stand against the tactics
of the Devil. For our battle is not against flesh and blood, but against
the rulers, against the authorities, against the world powers of this
darkness, against the spiritual forces of evil in the heavens. This is why
you must take up the full armor of God, so that you may be able to
resist in the evil day, and having prepared everything,
to take your stand. Stand, therefore,
with truth like a belt around your waist,
righteousness like armor on your chest,
and your feet sandaled with readiness for the gospel of peace.
In every situation take the shield of faith,
and with it you will be able to extinguish
the flaming arrows of the evil one.
Take the helmet of salvation,
and the sword of the Spirit, which is God's word.
With every prayer and request,
pray at all times in the Spirit, and stay alert in this,
with all perseverance and intercession for all the saints.
EPHESIANS 6:11–18 (EMPHASIS MINE)

PRAYER POINTS

- *Matthew 21:22*: "'And if you believe, you will receive whatever you ask for in prayer.'"

- *Luke 11:2–4*: "He said to them, 'Whenever you pray, say:
  Father,
  Your name be honored as holy.
  Your kingdom come.
  Give us each day our daily bread.
  And forgive us our sins,
  for we ourselves also forgive everyone in debt to us.
  And do not bring us into temptation.'"

PRAYER PROMPT

Come to the throne boldly! What have you been holding back in prayer from God? Present it to him now with confidence that he does hear and will answer.

PRAY

Heavenly Father, forgive me for holding onto my own problems so tightly. I realize now that you want me to bring you every care, every concern. You are my King, and all I have to do is enter into your throne room and present my needs in prayer. My desire is to do your will and teach the children you have put in my care. I can come to you when I am weary and burdened, and you will give me rest. I will learn from you, for you are gentle and humble in heart, and I will find rest for my soul. For your yoke is easy, and your burden is light! Amen.

Chapter 3
PRAY THE ISSUES
Student Behavior

Fathers, don't stir up anger in your children,
but bring them up in the training and instruction of the Lord.
EPHESIANS 6:4

"I don't have to listen to you!"

"What will you give me if I do this?"

Karen's head was swimming with the voices of her indignant students. It was the first week of school, and she had already lost her grip on her eighth graders. But then she wondered if she ever had a hold of them in the first place.

Assignments had become bargaining sessions. If you do this, I'll do that. Finish this first, and then we'll do this. On and on it went, day after day. She wasn't teaching; she was begging! Karen remembered that when she was in school, she'd never dare argue with her teacher about an assignment. The teacher had the last word. But not anymore.

Yet she noticed that these same students never seemed happy or content. There was no joy in learning. There was negotiation in its place. Karen had played this game before and lost. It was time for a different strategy.

"I've got a deal for you," she began. "You work, and you'll pass. You don't work, and you'll fail."

Simple yet satisfying.

Student behavior can be one of our greatest challenges as teachers. It can also be quite time consuming. A school's discipline program often doesn't come close to supporting teachers in the classroom—it ties teachers' hands instead. Parents hand over the care and concern of their children when the school bell rings. We become, in a sense, their parents for the next six hours or so. What should be our goal when it comes to student behavior? We must break the will without crushing the spirit. What an arduous task! How can we lead students to do what is right and at the same time impart wisdom? We must first become aware of the needs of all parties concerned. Only then can we pray effectively.

STUDENT BEHAVIOR

Students are children, and children require structure in order to feel safe and loved. Children also need to be noticed—to feel they are important to someone (don't we all?). Some children choose to act out in order to gain that much-desired attention; negative attention is better than no attention at all. Even those children who challenge our authority on a daily basis require the best of us. Even when we don't feel like loving them or they've done nothing to deserve our love, we must love them. Children are especially precious to our Lord. He told his disciples, "Leave the children alone, and don't try to keep them from coming to Me, because the kingdom of heaven is made up of people like this" (Matt. 19:14). That means that some of us stand in their way. Their greatest need is the love of Christ, not attention of the world but to be noticed by the King of heaven.

Our job, therefore, is more than maintaining discipline in the classroom. It is more than teaching students to be good citizens. It is more than any curriculum, any skill. Our job is to lead them to a saving knowledge of Christ by the way we teach. Some of us will be seed planters. Others will grow these tender seedlings. And still others will reap the harvest. With those especially difficult children you may be the seed planter. It may be years and years before you know the status of the seed you planted. In fact, you may never find out what happens to it. Remember that once the seed is planted, God does not forget about it. He will send someone to water it.

When I left teaching to stay at home with my two young boys, I felt very empty for a long time. I loved teaching. I loved having the opportunity to mold young lives. I knew that as a mother I had an even more awesome responsibility, but there's something about beginning the school year with students who don't know you or trust you and then ending the year knowing some of them so well they could be your own children.

That last year of teaching I had a particularly troublesome student in my eighth-grade class. For the first half of the year Jay slept through my class. No matter what I did, he wasn't interested. I tried sending him to the office. I tried giving him positive reinforcement. I even tried bribery. Nothing worked. I hated to admit it, but Jay seemed like a lost cause. Through it all, I treated him with respect and looked for ways to find the good in him. Toward the end of the year Jay kept himself awake during my class. He wasn't doing a lot of work, but he was alert and polite. To me that was a miracle in itself.

The year ended and so did my career as a full-time teacher. Four years later as I walked my youngest child to the library, Jay caught up with me. He slowed his jet black pickup truck and called out to me. It took a few seconds for me to realize who it was. He looked so polished, so "together." But once he took off his sunglasses, I could see his eyes—those eyes that finally opened to me at the end of his eighth-grade year. He'd graduated high school and was going on to become an architectural draftsman. I was impressed to say the least. "You were the only one who cared," he said before driving away. God allowed me a glimpse into Jay's life after me, so I could see that the seed I planted took root.

All of your students deserve your prayers, but those in your midst who are the most unteachable or unlovable need them more than the others. Commit today to pray for those students who you could easily classify as your enemy.

> *"But I tell you, love your enemies and*
> *pray for those who persecute you."*
>
> MATTHEW 5:44

It's easy to love and pray for those students who do exactly as you say and whose performance is praiseworthy. There is no reward in that. Commit yourself today to pray for those who cause you the most trouble.

PARENT BEHAVIOR

Difficult students are sometimes the result of difficult parents. Often the key to dealing with troublesome students is to win the favor of their parents. We can win their favor in many practical ways, but the spiritual aspect is much more powerful. Our actions and words will be pleasing to others if we first strive to please God in those things.

At times, however, it seems as though we cannot please a particular parent, and we become discouraged. God provides ways for us to deal with difficult people that will please him and point those people in his direction.

Rejoice in hope; be patient in affliction; be persistent in prayer.
Share with the saints in their needs; pursue hospitality.
Bless those who persecute you; bless and do not curse.
ROMANS 12:12–14

How often do our teachers' lounges fill with words of complaint against a demanding or problematic parent? We complain to other teachers because we know they understand our plight. But their advice sometimes can lead us down the wrong path, encouraging us to take control of the situation and respond in ways that do not please God. The temptation to allow our difficulties with a parent to influence how we treat their child in the classroom is real. We might find ourselves treating him more harshly or even ignoring his contributions because we are annoyed or angry at his parent. In the absence of godly counsel, we will listen to whatever advice we receive. Right now you will hear what God has to say. Cling to his counsel. Let's look at Romans 12:12–14 once more.

REJOICE IN HOPE

We can be easily discouraged when parents confront us about the decisions we make regarding their children—our students. If we strive to do all things to please God, we will please him with our decisions, with our words, with our actions, and with our attitudes. We can rejoice in the hope of God's glory—that is, we can be joyful right now because we have the hope of our eternal state with God in the future. The parents of our most difficult students need to see that hope in us. Then they will want to know the source of that hope. If you can allow God to love their difficult child through you, these parents will be so grateful. It will soften them toward you and make them more willing to hear what you have to say.

BE PATIENT IN AFFLICTION

Picture yourself sitting in a parent/teacher conference, patiently waiting for the parent to finish criticizing your work or your program. Sometimes a parent's criticism is warranted. At other times, however, it is not. You may find yourself wrongfully accused or suddenly abandoned when parents should stand behind you. Lack of support is one of a teacher's greatest frustrations. God says that if you suffer for doing good and you endure it, this is commendable before him (1 Pet. 2:20).

BE PERSISTENT IN PRAYER

If we rejoice in the hope we have in God, we will be more patient during trials; we won't pray in a lifeless manner or become weary. We will instead pray without ceasing by lifting up the needs of those put in our midst. Compared to their children, parents cross our paths infrequently, yet their influence in students' lives supercedes our own. We must pray continually for them as they guide their children.

SHARE WITH THE SAINTS IN THEIR NEEDS; PRACTICE HOSPITALITY

We may not always be aware of which of our student's parents are believers and which are not. Unfortunately Christians don't always reflect God to the world. Even though this verse specifically talks about practicing hospitality to fellow believers, God expects us to do good to all people. Parents of our students can seem like strangers to us. We are encouraged to practice hospitality to strangers. But right where we are, in our classrooms, we can "do good" to all those who enter. Be hospitable and accommodating to parents when they come to see you or call you on the phone.

> *Therefore, as we have opportunity, we must*
> *work for the good of all, especially for those who belong*
> *to the household of faith.*
> GALATIANS 6:10

BLESS THOSE WHO PERSECUTE YOU; BLESS AND DO NOT CURSE

Have you ever experienced an angry parent whose words hurt and offended you? We all have. The words sting, and sometimes it is all we can do not to crumble in front of the angry parent. During times of persecution, we must strive to do good to those who persecute us instead of responding in turn.

Bless comes from the Greek word *eulogeo,* which literally means "to speak well of; to praise, to celebrate with praises." We are called to extend complete goodwill, not bless them when we pray and curse them at other times. We are to bless them always and not curse them at all.

Find something praiseworthy to say about their child right from the beginning. One practical way to do this is to make positive parent phone calls at the beginning of every school year. Then when and if you require parent assistance in a difficult matter, you will have their cooperation. Be proactive and nurture your relationship with parents before you have to deal with something negative.

As we consider how to deal with difficult children in our classrooms, we must again look to see how God wants parents to deal with children. Since our society has abdicated much of parental responsibility to schools, we can and should take this responsibility seriously. Discipline is key, but we must first prepare ourselves for this great responsibility.

SPARE THE ROD AND SPOIL THE CHILD

When the wicked increase, rebellion increases,
but the righteous will see their downfall.
Discipline your son, and he will give you comfort;
he will also give you delight.
PROVERBS 29:16–17

You know whether you are a good disciplinarian. You know whether you are in control of your classroom. If you have difficulty in this area, then you are spending more time disciplining than you are teaching. Humble yourself and ask for help. We have precious little time with our students already; don't waste time avoiding the issue. Thank God for revealing your weakness and then pray for wisdom when dealing with your students. Pray for God to send someone to help you get things under control—for the sake of your students.

TEACHER PREPAREDNESS IS KEY

Let the message about the Messiah dwell richly among you, teaching
and admonishing one another in all wisdom, and singing psalms,
hymns, and spiritual songs, with gratitude in your hearts to God. And
whatever you do, in word or in deed, do everything in the name of the
Lord Jesus, giving thanks to God the Father through Him.
COLOSSIANS 3:16–17

Most teachers go through extensive training to become teachers. We get college degrees, we serve multiple internships, and we continually attend workshops to learn new strategies and brush up on old ones. All of this training leads us to believe that we are perfectly equipped for the job ahead. But our training is not complete without the Word of God dwelling richly within us. Without wisdom, how will we teach effectively? Without a personal knowledge of mercy and grace, how will we discipline effectively? It is a mistake to believe that we can do any good apart from God. We were given the gift of teaching, and when we do it so that God may be glorified, we will indeed teach well.

These children, our students, were specifically put in our care by God himself. You are an appointed authority in their lives. He desires that they not be hindered to come to him. You can be a light to your students and their parents. In everything you do or say, do it all to the glory of God. When you discipline your students, act swiftly and fairly. When you conference with their parents, speak with wisdom and grace. Pray that your words are aptly spoken and "seasoned with salt, so that you may know how you should answer each person" (Col. 4:6).

PRAYER POINTS

- *Mark 10:14:* "When Jesus saw it, He was indignant and said to them, 'Let the little children come to Me. Don't stop them, for the kingdom of God belongs to such as these.'"

PRAYER PROMPT

Has a student or parent recently attacked your position, your authority, or your person? Remember the sting of rejection that Jesus himself felt. He prayed for those who persecuted him. You can too!

PRAY

Heavenly Father, so often I refer to my students as if they were my own children. In many ways I feel like their parent. My duties must therefore include training and instruction but without fear, anxiety, or frustration. I am called to provide for them, love them, bless them, correct them, pray for them, but not to provoke them. In everything I must set an example by doing what is good. You discipline your children because you love them. My desire is to obey your precepts and commands. My greatest desire is to please you. Help me to lead my students toward the truth. Help me to stand firm when it is required. Let me show mercy when it is appropriate. Never let me lead my students astray by ignoring defiance or disobedience. It will shorten their lives and destroy their futures. Guide my words and my actions each day with regard to their behavior. Help me to be mindful of their strengths and weaknesses so that I might give them what they need. Help me also to teach in a way that is pleasing in order to build up my students and not tear them down. Amen.

Chapter 4

PRAY THE ISSUES

Relationships with Parents

Since you put away lying, Speak the truth, each one to his neighbor, because we are members of one another.
EPHESIANS 4:25

I remember the day our firstborn son started school. Christopher's enthusiasm matched my own. I loved school and wanted so much for my children to share in that love for learning. This first day of school, however, was not as I imagined it. I was teaching at Christopher's school and walking him to his kindergarten classroom just one hallway over from my own classroom. Nevertheless, I was nervous and more anxious than I expected. The hallway seemed to close in on us as we neared his class. It was filled with parents of kindergartners—some were crying uncontrollably, and others stood in silence alone.

Mrs. Sauri had taught kindergarten for ten years. She was a pro. Since I was new to this school, I didn't feel as though I had an edge at all. There would be no special treatment for Chris as a TK (teacher's kid). Maybe that was for the best. And from prior experience I knew that his attitude toward new situations was based largely on what he observed in me. If I showed anxiety, then he would be anxious. If I showed confidence, then he would be confident.

I was keenly aware of his little hand in mine as we entered the room. He started to pull away before I was ready, but he turned first to see if it was OK to go. My smile gave him the permission he sought, and he fled from me to his desk, where he recognized his perfectly printed name. Now I stood there in the middle of the room amongst all these little people and their parents feeling lost and alone. It was time to share my son with this teacher. It was the beginning of letting him go. What if I wasn't ready?

Mrs. Sauri recognized my look of fear and uncertainty and came over just in time.

"He's going to do fine," she assured me.

"I'm sure he will, but will I?" I said, only half joking.

"Peek in whenever you like," she said.

That's when I knew Christopher was in good hands, although not my own.

Throughout that year I did peek in on him. I smiled as he ran through the field behind my classroom during physical education. I gave him our secret I-Love-You signal when we passed in the cafeteria. I passed his classroom on my way to the front office even though it was out of my way just so I could quickly look through the tiny window in the door. He was doing just fine.

I always tried to partner with parents when I was a teacher, but that year I knew what it was like from both sides. Never underestimate the power of a mother's love. It's that love that will hopefully be transferred to you. *Parents as partners* is a phrase we hear often, but it can be difficult to realize in a practical sense. What does it mean to be in partnership? How do we need parents, and how do they need us? Our relationship with the parents of our students is one of the most essential relationships we have. We must nurture those relationships so that we can better nurture our relationships with students. Each child you serve has a parent you can pray for. You can't effectively pray for one without praying for the other.

PARTNERSHIP

There are different kinds of partnerships, but the one thing most partnerships have in common is that they exist by choice. Two people come together with similar beliefs and desires for a common purpose. That is the ideal partnership. However, since we live in a fallen world as fallen people, that ideal partnership is rarely found. As educators we talk a lot about the importance of partnering with parents, but neither side has a say in the arrangement. Children find themselves in our classrooms caught between teacher and parent when the children instead should be the common purpose for which both sides work. What makes a good partnership? How can we move closer to this ideal we all seek?

Some parent-teacher partnerships are silent partnerships—others are far from it. The silent partners believe that both parent and teacher have the same goals, and they trust that those goals will be met with little or no interference on their part. The less-than-silent partners don't believe you have the same goals and do not trust that their interests will be represented unless they make them loud and clear. Neither situation is the ideal. As you would expect, the ideal is somewhere between the two.

This is not to say that parents have no responsibility for the nurturing of a strong, positive partnership, but we can do our part by following a few simple guidelines:

- *Show Respect*—We can show respect for parents in the way we speak about them to others. We can show that same respect when we speak to them personally either informally or in a formal conference. It is tempting to complain about a parent while in the teachers' lounge. Choose instead to bridle your tongue and pray silently for the parent each time a complaint enters your mind.
- *Build Trust*—We can build trust by keeping conversations between parent and teacher confidential. We can make sure we get our information firsthand from parents and not from our students or other teachers. It takes extra time and effort to make that parent phone call, but your action tells a parent that you care enough to get the truth right from the source.
- *Provide Information*—If parents request specific information about their child or how to best help their child, we can provide that information in a timely and quality manner. We can volunteer information when the situation calls for it. I know school days are incredibly hectic, but if we promise to send something home, make a follow-up phone call, or find a resource for a parent, we need to honor that promise. Oftentimes when I don't hear back from teachers, it's not just that they are overwhelmed; it's because they are disorganized and have misplaced my request. When I know that, I can extend them grace; but if I don't know that, I assume they are ignoring me.
- *Pray*—We can pray that our students' parents will grow and mature; we can pray for their relationships with their children, for alleviation of household stress, and for wisdom when dealing with their children and school officials.

Parents who are involved in their child's education are faced with more things to worry about than those who are not. Pray also that you will be a source of wisdom to them. Pray that the Holy Spirit will guide your tongue and choose your words for you during every conversation or conference.

RECIPROCAL RELATIONSHIP

The relationship between teachers and parents is a reciprocal one—it is mutually beneficial, or it can be. We need parents to parent in a way that fosters school success. We also need them to support our position of authority in their children's lives. Finally, we need them to provide us with any additional information necessary for us to meet the specific needs of their children. But this is a two-way street. Parents need us to give their children the attention they need in order to succeed in school. They need us to respect their position of authority in the lives of our students. And they need us to offer them a place on our team!

Keep in mind that even though this is a reciprocal relationship, there is no guarantee that either side will keep up its end of the agreement. In fact, when parents don't do their part, it is a source of great frustration and even discouragement to teachers. Similarly, when we don't do our part as teachers, we frustrate and discourage parents. If you discover that a parent is also a Christian, you may think you will experience smooth sailing in your relationship with that parent. That isn't always the case. Our expectations are higher for the Christian parent, and their expectations are higher for us as Christian teachers. One of my most disappointing experiences with my son was when he was in second grade. One of his teachers professed to be a Christian. I was thrilled—at first. I made the mistake of thinking that if she were a Christian, then she was also close to perfect. Her decisions, actions, and words toward our son continually disappointed and frustrated me. I tried to approach her with love, but she became defensive and angry. Although my outside response was above reproach, I began to harbor bitterness toward her in my heart.

Since that time I have asked God to reveal in me whatever sin got in the way of that relationship with a sister in Christ—my own pride as a former teacher is what got in the way. Now that our son is in middle school, I tread lightly and gently with teachers. So when a teacher lets parents know she is in need of volunteers, I respond with, "How can I best serve you in your classroom?" That doesn't always guarantee a reciprocal relationship, but it helps. As a teacher I need to have the same attitude toward parents, "How can I best serve you?" A humble heart is required.

Nurture Versus Nature

The debate of nurture versus nature is never more evident than in the classroom. Educational psychologists tend to come down on the side of "nurture" as the defining influence in a child's life, thereby placing the influence of the teacher at a definite advantage over that of the parent. If you've spent any time as a classroom teacher, however, you know how powerfully a child's home life dictates his success in your classroom. For the purpose of this discussion, I define "nature" as home life and not genetic code.

When I taught at a school in the inner city of Tampa, Florida, I was told by our principal not to come early or stay late, not to bring anything of value to school, and if I could help it, not to drive a nice car to park in the parking lot. I taught learning disabled students, and many of my students lived in the projects that surrounded the school. No matter what progress I thought we made during the school day, it seemed to be undone between the hours of 4:00 P.M. and 8:00 A.M. the next day. My students' nights and weekends were full of the sounds of sirens, gunshots, backstreet brawls, and sometimes bedroom battering. Some went to bed hungry. Others roamed the streets until the wee hours of the morning. Trying to teach with hope they would retain any of it was like trying to fill a pail full of holes with water.

I learned then how crucial a stable, nurturing home life was to the success of my students. But somehow when we are faced with very involved parents, we back away, afraid they will tell us how to run our classrooms. Due to our territorial nature, we don't respond well to *outsiders* telling us what to do. Unfortunately, with our defenses up we may never realize the power a positive parent can add to our classroom and our work as teachers. The majority of parents do not understand the culture of a school and will blunder through trying to gain help for their child. Admittedly, many are overprotective and overzealous in their quest. Even when my own son began school, I had to learn how to communicate effectively with his teachers without overwhelming them. I made numerous mistakes before I learned those lessons. Today I try to give their teachers a lot of room to work with my child before I charge in like the cavalry. I think I would have learned faster if the teachers had given me needed insight instead of stiffening like a brick wall when I asked questions.

If parental relations are a challenge for you, pray that God will reveal to you your own weakness first. He is faithful and will do just that. The prophet Jeremiah prayed for this himself.

> "I know, LORD,
> that a man's way of life is not his own;

> *no one who walks determines his own steps.*
> *Discipline me, Lord, but with justice—*
> *not in Your anger,*
> *or You will reduce me to nothing."*
> JEREMIAH 10:23–24

Rest assured that God will correct you, but he will do it with justice, not out of anger. Be willing to accept his correction, for God corrects only those he loves. We are sons and daughters of the King, and we are called to walk as such. Discipline should render us more dependent on God—it should cause us to turn to him. If you struggle with a difficult parent, pray first that God will reveal to you any fault of your own. Then pray that the parent's heart will be softened toward you, so that he or she can receive God's love poured out on them through you. Be persistent in your prayers for parents. Sometimes you may feel as though injustice has been done against you. Bring it to the Lord in prayer. Cry out to him. But then leave your complaint at the foot of the cross and go forward in love to serve your students.

PRAYER POINTS

- *1 Peter 2:17:* "Honor everyone. Love the brotherhood. Fear God. Honor the Emperor."
- *Philippians 2:3:* "Do nothing out of rivalry or conceit, but in humility consider others as more important than yourselves."

PRAYER PROMPT

Sometimes when we see a student struggling or hurting, there's a good chance there is a struggling or hurting parent at home. Even if you've not been made aware of a home issue, pray for the parents of those who struggle in your classroom.

PRAY

Lord, I am humbled as I realize that I have not been able to give my students all they need and deserve. I was blinded with pride that I was the best person for the job. The love of a mother can never be replaced. But for those with no mother's love, let me fill their need. For those with loving mothers, let me only add to their expertise. Help me to know when I should stop and when I should go. Help me to know my weakness in this and all areas. Only then will I become completely dependent upon you. I will remember that anything good I do, I can do because you made me capable. I desire to inspire my students, not discourage them. I want always to be compassionate. Show me how! Amen.

*"Blessed are the merciful,
because they will be shown mercy.
Blessed are the pure in heart,
because they will see God.
Blessed are the peacemakers,
because they will be called sons of God."*

MATTHEW 5:7–9

I've been a "new" teacher more than once. I was new as a first-year teacher. I was new when I changed schools to work closer to my home. And I was new when I returned to the classroom after a five-year absence.

When I transferred to a school closer to my home, replacing my two-hour daily commute, I was thrilled. I was now within walking distance of school. But being the "new teacher" had its own host of concerns. I knew no one at this school, and getting to know the culture of a school is no easy task. There were secret, unwritten rules that I didn't know about until I broke them. I needed a mentor. I needed a guide. I found one on that very first day in Diane Williams.

Diane also taught learning disabled students. We were on the special education team together. Her classroom was right across the hall from my own. And here was the best part—Diane was a Christian. I praised God for this blessing. I believed everything would be OK.

Diane certainly knew the ropes. She knew who held the power and who didn't at our school. She knew how to get the workroom aide to make copies for her when she needed them—something I needed to learn quickly. She knew who to trust and who to avoid. She knew how to go to bat for our students when no one else would. But Diane had a flaw, one that I didn't uncover soon enough. Diane was not well liked at our school.

Many of our colleagues were uneasy around her. She was very critical and not at all quiet about her opinions of how others did their jobs. She was aggressive in her quest for excellence, and it alienated her from the rest of the faculty. And now I was her new best friend. That alienated me from the faculty as well.

I knew I needed to talk to Diane, but I didn't trust my own motives. Was it because I was worried about my own reputation? Was it because I was worried about Diane's reputation? Yes, on both counts. But then the Holy Spirit nudged me to the most important reason—it was God's reputation on the line that mattered. Everyone in our school knew Diane and I were Christians, and right now Diane wasn't a sweet aroma to that faculty. I prayed for two weeks about how and when to confront Diane. I prayed that

God would soften her heart toward me and that she would have ears to hear.

I did finally talk to Diane. She was stunned into silence. It took a few days for her to talk to me again. And when she did, she responded with grace and thanks. I was incredibly relieved.

Teaching is all about relationships, and the relationships we cultivate with other teachers can either foster or hinder our success in the classroom. We can't control how others respond or react to any given situation, but we can control how *we* respond and react. Our responsibility to these relationships is to be merciful, pure in heart, and peacemakers. Concentrate on these three areas, and your interactions with colleagues will flourish in a way that blesses you and your students. Pray daily that your words and actions will display mercy, purity, and peace.

BLESSED BE

The Beatitudes talk about God's blessing on his people who exhibit certain character traits. Usually "blessed" refers to God himself, but in this context "blessed" refers to blessings from God to man. Our relationships with others are dependent upon our character. Three of these Beatitudes apply to our character while we're in relationship with other teachers. We would do well to focus on these traits. Character education isn't just for students. We must set our hearts first on our own character development. Then we can work on that of our students.

> *But each person should examine his own work,*
> *and then he will have a reason for boasting in himself*
> *alone, and not in respect to someone else. For each person*
> *will have to carry his own load.*
> GALATIANS 6:4–5

BE MERCIFUL

"The merciful are happy. We must not only bear our own afflictions patiently, but we must do all we can to help those who are in misery. We must have compassion on the souls of others, and help them; pity those who are in sin, and seek to snatch them as brands out of the burning."[1]

To show mercy is to show compassion toward others. Look around during your lunchtime at school. You will see some who are in misery. They no longer can find the good in what they do. You will see others who are struggling to stay in their jobs. They are discouraged and disillusioned. You will see those who make the wrong choices or use the wrong words with students. They are bitter and often angry about what they do each day. Having lunch with any of these kinds of teachers may lead you instead to eat in your classroom. I encourage you to see them for who they really are—broken people God has put in your midst to love.

As you see a teacher whose attitude is one of chronic pessimism, find out what that person really needs and offer help. It may be as simple as a shoulder to cry on. You may want to offer solutions to the problems, but do so only when asked. Instead look for the positive in her classroom and compliment her on it. It may help her shift her focus.

I remember one "veteran" teacher who almost never smiled. She always complained, whether it was about the students, their parents, our new principal, or district mandates. At first I thought she'd been teaching too long and was in need of a sabbatical. Initially I avoided her table at lunch because I didn't want to waste my precious twenty minutes away from the classroom listening to her constant complaining. Somehow it was the only available seating each day, and so I sat and listened. Finally I decided that if I was going to sit with her, I might as well find out more about her. So I started asking questions.

Questions about her family. Questions about where she grew up. Questions about why and how she became a teacher. After a while, our conversations revolved around common interests instead of common complaints. And when I left to have my first child, she was the one who crocheted the most gorgeous baby blanket and cried at my leaving. I made a good friend that year—one I wouldn't have made had there been an empty seat at another table.

We show mercy when it's not deserved—that's what makes it so powerful.

BE PURE IN HEART

"The pure in heart are happy; for they shall see God. Here holiness and happiness are fully described and put together. The heart must be purified by faith, and kept for God. Create in me such a clean heart, O God. None but the pure are capable of seeing God, nor would heaven be happiness to the impure. As God cannot endure to look upon their iniquity, so they cannot look upon his purity."[2]

A pure heart is one that has God in the center of it and seeks him above all else. If you have a pure heart, it is easier to avoid the temptation to fall in with the complaining spirits of others, to speak as the unwise do, or to act in a way unbefitting a son or daughter of the King. There were many instances in which I was teased—yes, even by other teachers—about being such a "good girl." Conversations stopped midsentence when I approached. Certain jokes weren't told in my presence. But I came to realize that was not a bad thing. My goal was not to make others feel uncomfortable but to protect God's reputation. After all, if I belong to him, my actions and words should reflect on his character.

A pure heart is also a forgiving heart. A pure heart avoids "foolish and ignorant disputes, . . . but must be gentle to everyone, able to teach, and patient" (2 Tim. 2:23–24). It can be difficult to sit in a committee meeting and listen while others act and speak foolishly. That happens in every profession and at almost every gathering. Once people see that you have a pure heart, they will know that you do not have an agenda like most people and that they can trust you to always speak the truth. Such qualities only improve relationships, not harm them.

BE A PEACEMAKER

"The peacemakers are happy. They love, and desire, and delight in peace; and study to be quiet. They keep the peace that it be not broken, and recover it when it is broken. If the peacemakers are blessed, woe to the peace-breakers!"[3]

My sister, Amy, is the middle child in our family. Her role, according to popular birth-order books, is one of peacemaker. She was and continues to be the defender of the defenseless and a righter of wrongs. Injustice doesn't stand a chance with Amy around! School settings are particularly liable to claims of injustice and inequity. Parents accuse teachers of unfair treatment or partiality. Teachers attack other teachers because they have different teaching styles. Gossip runs rampant from the teachers' lounge. Sometimes it's not the student's squabbles we find ourselves in the middle of—it's our own!

A peacemaker is someone after God's own heart; after all, Jesus came to bring peace between man and God. It takes a certain amount of self-sacrifice, forbearance, and a willingness to build others up (edification) to be an effective peacemaker. In order to do things the way that pleases God (the only way to bring peace), we must deny ourselves—that is, to deny our own importance, desires, and will. Jesus said, "If anyone wants to come with Me, he must deny himself, take up his cross, and follow Me. For whoever wants to save his life will lose it, but whoever loses his life because of Me will find it" (Matt. 16:24–25). We can sacrifice "our way" in order for others to have their way. We can sacrifice "our time" to give time to others. We can sacrifice "our position or platform" to advance the platform of another—if we desire to bring peace.

Forbearance means "to endure one another's burdens." That may mean to listen and sympathize. This is especially true when working with other Christians. "Walk worthy of the calling you have received, with all humility and gentleness, with patience, accepting one another in love, diligently keeping the unity of the Spirit with the peace that binds [us]" (Eph. 4:1b–3). It doesn't hurt to extend this "accepting one another in love" to those who do not yet know Christ. It may be the very thing the Spirit uses to draw them to himself.

We are all in desperate need of encouragement. Teachers are especially impoverished in this area. We can wait until society wakes up and realizes how brokenhearted some of us are, or we can take it upon ourselves to encourage one another. Who else but another teacher knows the frustrations, joys, disillusionment, and pleasures of being a teacher? We are each strong in our own ways and can help those who are weak because of it. Our goal should be to build one another up, not to tear one another down. Paul expressed it this way in Romans 15:1–2: "Now we who are strong have an obligation to bear the weaknesses of those without strength, and not to please ourselves. Each one of us must please his neighbor for his good, in order to build him up." How do we build up one another? We do it with our words. Choose only words that are helpful according to the needs of others (Eph. 4:29).

Our relationships with other teachers affect our students. What do you say if a student comes to you with a complaint about another teacher? How do you respond? What you say will determine how that student now views that teacher. Measure your words carefully at all times. Make sure that what you say and do is merciful. Make sure that your motives are always to please God and to know him better. Embrace your God-given role as peacemaker. Let your prayers be out of humbleness of heart for the encouragement of others. Allow God to use you as an instrument of his peace.

Prayer Points

- *Proverbs 14:21:*
  "The one who despises his neighbor sins,
  but whoever shows kindness to the poor will be happy."
- *Luke 6:36:* "'Be merciful, just as your Father also is merciful.'"

Prayer Prompt

Is there a teacher you are avoiding right now? Or someone whose style of teaching, classroom organization, or discipline rubs you the wrong way? Take it as a prodding of the Holy Spirit to pray for that person. Then meekly, with all humility, be the peacemaker you are called to be.

Pray

Lord, it is impossible to please everyone. Someone is always disappointed no matter what I do. But now there are a few who seek to discredit me and drive me away from my position. They do not know you, Lord. But they do know that I know you, and it makes them angry. Help me to focus on being a sweet smell to those around me. Let me not be ashamed of my faith in you. Draw others to yourself in an obvious way. And help me to do all things in a way that pleases you. Those ways will please others as well. Amen.

Chapter 6

PRAY THE ISSUES

Submitting to Authority

Submit to every human institution because of the Lord, whether to the Emperor as the supreme authority, or to governors as those sent out by him to punish those who do evil and to praise those who do good. For it is God's will that you, by doing good, silence the ignorance of foolish people. As God's slaves, [live] as free people, but don't use your freedom as a way to conceal evil. Honor everyone. Love the brotherhood. Fear God. Honor the Emperor.

1 PETER 2:13–17

I believe that we are all basically still in high school. I was never more reminded of this than when I attended school faculty meetings. Sitting in our middle school auditorium, it was easy to identify all the cliques. The jocks (our P.E. Department and many of the male teachers), the nerds (our highly intellectual teachers of advanced classes), and the popular crowd (the "beautiful" people and those with the gift of being a student favorite) all sat together. Then there were the rest of us. Those who didn't dress according to the trends (still wearing the same outfit only popular in 1975), those who were painfully shy and who sat alone during lunch, and those who just didn't know where they belonged (me). I remember cringing during my first faculty meeting as a brand-new teacher when I realized nothing had changed! And then there were those who bucked authority at every turn. They were usually found together as well, in meetings, during lunch, and huddled in the hallways during their assigned duty.

One of the greatest challenges to a faculty is losing a principal and then getting a new one. It can be a very painful process, and many teachers can be lost during this transition. Lines are drawn and schools split between those who support the new principal and those who do not. It is really a matter of submitting to the authority God places in our lives, but somehow that truth doesn't seem as clear in the context of a school.

I watched one year when we got a new principal how the auditorium visibly shifted from one faculty to two. I couldn't imagine being that principal, whose desire was to bring unity to a fractured faculty and a quality education to its students. There were now more obstacles than anticipated. It was a hard place to be.

Teachers are very independent thinkers. We've already discussed how territorial we can be, so it's no surprise that authority figures can be a challenge for us. The enemy would have us rebel and rely only on our expert status, but that's a temptation we can't afford to give in to. How we submit to authority is quite observable. Not only do those in authority watch our responses, but so do our colleagues, our students, and even their parents. Those teachers with less experience learn from our actions, choices, and reactions. Our students hear us if we say something against either another teacher or the principal. Their respect for authority follows our own. We must be in prayer about and for those in authority over us.

How much effort do you put into your relationship with your principal or other authority figures in your career? Remember that he or she is there to help you and needs your cooperation and support. Respect for authority is a character trait missing among many of our students. Even though our own authority as teachers seems to have diminished, we must not allow ourselves to be less submissive to the authorities God himself has placed in our lives. Principals, team leaders, committee chairs, district supervisors, and the superintendent are all appointed as authorities over us as teachers. Be willing to give Caesar what is Caesar's and God what is God's (Matt. 22:21). The only exception to submission is when any of those authorities ask you to sin.

RESPECT, HONOR, OBEY, AND SUBMIT

All of our relationships—not only our marriages—should be based on the four words above. They are all closely related, with a few minor differences. *Respect* is defined as "to look away from all else to one object."[1] In a marriage we are to look away from all others and only to our spouse. In school we are to look away from the negative influences of others and only to our principal. Obviously our principals and other administrators are flawed people and don't always make the right choices, but by their very position they deserve our respect. When things go wrong in a school, teachers tend to huddle together against the administration. One of our greatest mistakes is thinking the principal is "one of them" when, in fact, he or she is "one of us." Principals should be seen as "lead" teachers. Treat them with respect from that viewpoint, and they may surprise you.

Honor and *respect* sometimes are interchanged, but *honor* has a meaning all its own. According to *Vine's Expository Dictionary*, *honor* means "to esteem or value above oneself."[2] We are called to give honor to all to whom it is due. Honor is due our principals and administrators. It is within God's design of headship that they receive honor.

To *obey* means to "listen and attend."[3] Once in a while we find ourselves in a faculty meeting, and when the principal says something about an issue with which we disagree, we "tune him out." We don't listen. And sometimes when we do listen, we don't attend to what we heard. In other words, we hear what he has to say; we might even respond with "Yes," but then we do not follow through with what we have been told. Think of a time when a student or your own child has responded to a command with, "Yes, Mom or Mrs. So and So," but then proceeded to do what they wanted anyway, disregarding what we asked them to do. It has been said that teachers can make or break a principal or a program. As a Christian teacher, I encourage you to "make" that principal.

Submission is a controversial term in today's society. Literally it means to "retire, withdraw."[4] If we are to submit to God's will and God's will is that we submit to the appointed authorities in our lives, then we need to submit to them. At times teachers may be known to dig in their heels on minor issues. Sometimes we react that way because we feel it is our right; sometimes, because we disagree philosophically with our authorities. But many times it is because of pride. I remember one principal who forbade me to take my students on a particular field trip. He wouldn't explain himself, and I couldn't see any logical reason why I couldn't. I became frustrated and then angry that he wasn't being reasonable. I remember complaining about it to my husband, who said, "Is he asking you to sin?"

"No, of course not," I said.

"Then leave it alone; withdraw," he said.

I was being called to submit—to retreat. Even though I couldn't see any good reason not to go on the field trip, that doesn't mean there wasn't one. And if there wasn't one, it didn't matter. What mattered was that God used this situation to purify me and to protect his own reputation. My principal knew I was a Christian. What kind of message would I have sent had I not submitted to his authority?

We don't always see the "big" picture in our everyday lives. Our willingness to submit to authority is a picture of our willingness to submit to God's authority in our lives. In raising our own children, my husband and I taught them that obedience was determined by a three-pronged test: (1) Did you do what I asked you to do? (2) Did you do it right away? (3) Did you do it with a happy spirit? Have you ever found yourself doing what your administrator asked you to do within the necessary time frame, yet grumbling under your breath the whole time? If we have a heart for obedience and submission, we will respond willingly out of ultimate respect and honor for our Father in heaven. Respect, honor, obey, and submit to the God-given authorities in your life, and you will be blessed.

VERSES REGARDING RESPECT, HONOR, OBEY, AND SUBMIT

Since we are one of the God-appointed authorities in the lives of our students, it is crucial that we model for them how to respect, honor, obey, and submit. The Bible has much to say about these topics. They are key to both the joy we seek in serving and the future joys our students can experience.

> *My son, fear the LORD, as well as the king,*
> *and don't associate with rebels,*
> *for their destruction will come suddenly;*
> *who knows what disaster these two can bring?*

PROVERBS 24:21–22

Early in this chapter I included a story about a teacher trying to find her way with a new principal. It is based loosely on one of my own experiences. But in my experience many of the other teachers collectively chose to ignore the new principal's request to write goals for the year. They acted in defiance of her authority. Two distinct camps began to grow—one in support of the new principal and one in rebellion to her. A line was drawn in the sand. Lunchroom conversations revolved around topics such as "Who does she think she is?" or "We'll see how long she lasts" or "If things don't change around here, I'm transferring to another school!" Eventually the roaring fire of the dissidents flickered out, and many did transfer at the end of the year. They left jobs they had for many years in favor of starting over at a new school. They lost any seniority they had and all relationships. Who knows if their new school and its principal were any better? They may have jumped from the frying pan right into the fire. I'm just grateful I was able to look away from all others and keep my eyes on one thing—the truth. The truth is that my principal had been appointed over me, and I was to fearfully remember who put her where she was in my life.

Remind them to be submissive to rulers and authorities, to obey,
to be ready for every good work, to slander no one, to avoid fighting,
and to be kind, always showing gentleness to all people.
TITUS 3:1–2

One of the greatest sources of strife between administrators and teachers in my district was the fact that administrators told us there was no money, yet at the same time they had built a new administration building, which teachers referred to as the Taj Mahal. No wonder there was no money available for teacher pay increases or textbooks or supplies, we assumed. Teachers became bitter, and each time new training was required at that building, we found different ways to avoid it. The rift between supervisors and teachers grew, and teacher morale suffered. One summer I worked as an administrative assistant in the Taj Mahal. It didn't take long for me to see just how frustrated and discouraged the supervisors were. They were overworked, understaffed, overwhelmed, and underappreciated. They had more in common with teachers than any of us realized. I gained a new appreciation for those working there that summer and took it upon myself to educate other teachers about the realities of working in the Taj Mahal. Yet God wants us to be considerate and peaceable and do what is good whether or not we know the real story. The following verse is a command; there is no condition attached.

> *Submit to every human institution because of the Lord, whether to the Emperor as the supreme authority, or to governors as those sent out by him to punish those who do evil and to praise those who do good. For it is God's will that you, by doing good, silence the ignorance of foolish people. As God's slaves, [live] as free people, but don't use your freedom as a way to conceal evil. Honor everyone.*
> *Love the brotherhood. Fear God. Honor the Emperor.*

1 PETER 2:13–17

This verse is as inclusive as any verse regarding our responsibility to God-given authorities. It puts to rest any of our questions or struggles with how to respond to our team leaders or administrators. Submit yourselves to them! Peter said that it is God's will that by doing good toward and for the authorities in our lives, we will silence any ignorant talk from those who are foolish. I know that even when I clash with the personality of someone who is my "boss," I am obligated to submit to them anyway and show the proper respect. When students used to come to me and complain about another teacher, I told them not to let a personality conflict get in the way of their learning. It is their job to do what is right regardless. The same can be said for us as we have difficulties with anyone who is in authority over us as teachers. Don't let a personality conflict get in the way of doing what is right.

Obey your leaders and submit to them, for they keep watch
over your souls as those who will give an account, so that they can do
this with joy and not with grief, for that would be unprofitable for you.
HEBREWS 13:17

Even though this verse speaks of church elders, treating our administrators with the same respect improves even difficult situations. Too often we look at our principals as aloof, uninvolved administrators when in fact they agonize over the performance of their teachers just as we agonize over the performance of our students. When an administrator encounters a teacher who is in defiance of their authority, they are sometimes at a loss about how to handle the situation—just as we sometimes feel powerless to deal effectively with a defiant student. It can be a discouraging and disappointing job. I encourage parents to think the best of teachers—that their intentions are honorable, that they go into teaching because they love children and desire to make a lasting impact on their lives. In the same way, I encourage teachers to think the best of their principals. Yes, there are those who go into educational leadership for power, but more often they believe they are gifted with the expertise necessary to improve education for all children. They want to widen their circle of influence and reach more children than they could in their own classrooms. Just as no parent or teacher is perfect, neither are principals. But it is part of our job to make their job easier, not more difficult. It is their job to watch over our performance as teachers because they must give account to authorities above them for it. Their accountability as leaders reaches to the highest authority over us all. Even though our students don't always obey us in order to make our jobs easier, we nevertheless should strive to ease the burden for our principals. Making life more difficult for them does not make life easier for us.

There is one exception to all these commands and guidelines. If your principal insists on obedience to a demand that would lead you into sin, you are under the umbrella of God's protection to disobey. Even though a principal's expectations or commands seem illogical or ill advised, that does not mean they are sinful. Consider carefully your reasons for disobedience; make sure they don't indicate defiance instead. We don't always get our way. Sometimes we think a principal's authority dilutes our own, when, in fact, it is in place to support our authority in the lives of students. Keep your eyes on God as you serve your principal. Serve as a bond servant to his master. After all, you are under contract. Pray for a willing spirit and for protection over your principal. He or she is in this battle with you.

PRAYER POINTS

- *1 Peter 5:5–6:* "Likewise, you younger men, be subject to the elders. And all of you clothe yourselves with humility toward one another, because

    God resists the proud,

    but gives grace to the humble.

    Humble yourselves therefore under the mighty hand of God, so that He may exalt you in due time."

- *Romans 13:1–2:* "Everyone must submit to the governing authorities, for there is no authority except from God, and those that exist are instituted by God. So then, the one who resists the authority is opposing God's command, and those who oppose it will bring judgment on themselves."

- *Romans 13:7:* "Pay your obligations to everyone: taxes to those you owe taxes, tolls to those you owe tolls, respect to those you owe respect, and honor to those you owe honor."

PRAYER PROMPT

You probably are unaware of your principal's daily struggles, his prayers, his dreams for his teachers and his students. Commit to pray for him today and every day that he will be a godly master and that you will be a faithful servant.

PRAY

Lord, sometimes it is hard to distinguish between submitting to the authority you have placed above me and doing the right thing. I may choose to overlook a wrong because of grace. But others may overlook it to protect their own image. You see everything, Lord. You know where things are hidden, and you know the motives of the heart. Shine your light on those things which are hidden. Reveal the motives of those who seek their own glory. Reveal my own motives and purge my heart of any defiance. Protect me as I pursue the truth of the matter. Bless me with your loving-kindness and vindicate me if necessary. Keep my eyes on you as I follow the one you have put as an authority in my life. Amen.

Chapter 7
PRAY THE ISSUES
Disappointment
~

There is nothing better for man than to eat,
drink, and to enjoy his work. I have seen that even
this is from God's hand. For who can eat and who
can enjoy life apart from Him?
ECCLESIASTES 2:24–25

The principal reason men and women go into teaching is to make a difference in the life of a child. This may not be true for all teachers, but it is true for most. We come into this profession with incredible expectations. We believe we can make a difference. We believe that we will have what we need to make a difference. And we believe everyone around us will support our attempts to make this difference. Our expectations are often not met, and the result is frustration and disappointment. This was certainly true for me each and every year I taught.

My very first teaching assignment was in what was then called a sixth-grade center. Only sixth graders attended this school as an attempt to relieve overcrowding in the traditional elementary schools in our area. As a special education teacher I was thrilled that I had only one grade to teach (one prep instead of five). To me it was a gift that would allow me to focus on the needs of the children in my charge. My training as a special education teacher prepared me to work in small, intimate groups of students. Unfortunately, I had three classes of twenty students! Disappointment number one.

Throughout the year I ran into one frustration after another. It is part of our job as teachers to solve the unexpected and unwelcome problems. The challenge was to maintain a sense of purpose and some idealistic enthusiasm in the middle of continuous obstacles.

Many things in our daily lives as teachers disappoint us. We experience disappointment when our expectations are not met. We become disappointed over our students' performance. We become disappointed over the behavior of others. We become disappointed over our own behavior. When God is disappointed, the Holy Spirit is grieved. Disappointment is allowable, if only for the moment. But we should not allow it to fester and turn into bitterness. God's gift to us is that we may find satisfaction in our work. Don't let disappointment steal that satisfaction from you. We can recognize each disappointment as an opportunity to pray in thanksgiving and then seek God's will in each situation.

GREAT EXPECTATIONS

I graduated with a teaching degree in Specific Learning Disabilities. I chose this field because I thought I could make a difference. All of my training worked through the model of individual or small-group instruction. I was very excited about working with children on that level. My first teaching job was in an inner-city ghetto. I must admit that I was disappointed in its setting. I was also disappointed that I had virtually no budget to speak of. But my greatest disappointment came when I had a class full of fifteen and sometimes twenty severely learning-disabled students. Individualized instruction quickly became an unattainable dream.

My job expectations were determined by what I knew to be true—that is, what my teacher preparation taught me. Disappointment commonly comes from our teacher preparation. College and university programs don't always teach according to "real world" scenarios. They teach according to the ideal. But disappointment can also come from unrealistic expectations we may have—the romanticized idea of teaching we envision before we have our first classroom. We picture our room as more than adequately equipped, with just the right amount of students, a principal who loves us as well as parents and other teachers who love us—oh, and society reveres our position!

Is it foolish to have high expectations? No. Every teacher learned about the "self-fulfilling prophecy" in students. If a child expects to do poorly, there is a strong chance he will do poorly. The same can be said for teachers. If we expect very little from those around us, most likely we'll receive very little. Certain personalities are more optimistic while others are more pessimistic. But God wants us to expect the best, from him and from others. When we pray, we sometimes forget to seek the best for our students, their parents, our colleagues, and ourselves. Things don't change because we do not ask God or when we do ask we ask with the wrong motives (James 4:2–3). Let us ask about all these things in the confidence that if we believe, God will give us what we seek.

STUDENT PERFORMANCE

As teachers we are always concerned with our students' performance. We worry about the children who don't seem to achieve no matter what we do. We are concerned about their futures—will they grow into successful, happy adults? Will their next teacher be able to make a difference? Even before the age of school accountability, teachers had high hopes for their students. We are disappointed when they don't do well with us. Oftentimes we are disappointed that the physical makeup of the class is what hinders achievement. If our classes are too large, we can't give the necessary attention to individual learning needs. If our classes are overly burdened with students with great emotional or behavioral needs, we spend most of our time maintaining order instead of teaching. If our classes are housed in a building in desperate need of repair or with poor air quality, no one can concentrate as well as they would in a better environment. We can have our high expectations, but too often reaching them is out of our control. When things feel out of our control, disappointment can easily turn into discouragement.

Our students deserve our very best. If we are disappointed with their performance, we must first check our own. Maybe we've been too distracted by our mountain of paperwork or a task assigned by one of our numerous committees or by our personal lives. Pray that God will give us the focus we need in order to teach well. Maybe we're not as prepared as we should be. Maybe we're out of our element— teaching something we are not equipped to teach well. If that is the case, pray for wisdom and guidance. If there is something we can do to improve student performance, we must do it. Sometimes that means asking for help. We don't have to do any of this alone.

Behavior of Others

No matter how many behavior management courses we took in college, we can't always control the behavior of others. People will disappoint us. How we respond to their behavior is what really matters.

STUDENTS

Have you ever had a substitute in your classroom? Of course, you have; we all have. Even if you usually effectively manage your students' behavior, they suddenly forget how to behave properly when you're absent. It can be very discouraging to come back after an illness to a not-so-flattering note about your students. The misbehavior of students is probably one of a teacher's greatest challenges. Because respect for teachers has diminished, it is more difficult than ever before to get students to behave. The energy it takes to maintain control is like one person trying to hold back a dam break. We all need help at one time or another.

No matter how challenging their students may be, many teachers are able to bring harmony to their classrooms. They may be veteran teachers who from their years of experience have figured out how to break the will of students without crushing their spirits. Their students love them. They are fair. They are structured. They are fun. Sometimes our disappointment in student behavior is tied to our own failings as a behavior manager. If this is the case, break out and ask for help from someone whose classroom is a delight to be in. Maybe you're that person in the life of another teacher. Be approachable. Be open to share what you've learned with others.

At times, however, no matter how good we are at what we do, a student's behavior can surprise and sometimes frighten us. I remember the day a chair came hurtling at me from across the room. It was thrown by a short-for-his-age seventh grader whose anger was bigger than he was. It was unexpected and frightening. I was devastated emotionally after I got home that evening. I never wanted to teach again if this was what I could expect. It was an isolated incident, but somehow it affected me so deeply that I questioned my choice of profession. I racked my brain trying to think of what I might have done wrong to deserve such treatment. Later I realized that no one deserves such treatment and that some children, no matter what we do, will never be what we expect them to be.

If students disappoint you with their behavior, look to make sure you are doing everything you can to "catch them being good" first. Then let go of that disappointment and look for ways or advice from other teachers about how to improve the situation. If a student has wronged you in some way, choose not to harbor ill feelings toward him so that you can walk forward doing whatever you can to improve his chances in this life.

PARENTS

Not every parent is as involved in their child's education as you would expect them to be. My first Open House night when I taught sixth grade in the inner city was a major disappointment. No one showed up—no one at all. The classroom was neat and completely decorated with students' work. I had sign-up sheets for volunteer needs and conferences. I had an award for the most improved student—but no one came. I couldn't believe that parents didn't care enough to come to Open House. At least that was my perception on that night.

We expect parents to be respectful. We expect parents to support our efforts with their children. We are often disappointed. We all have our share of parent stories to tell. Much of our disappointment is wrapped up in our perceptions. I perceived that parents did not care enough to come to my Open House. What I discovered was that in comparison to their everyday lives, Open House was not a high priority on their lists. Staying safe at night was. Wondering if they had enough food for breakfast the next day was. Keeping their children off the streets was. Sometimes we get so wrapped up in our own world that we can't see past what is important to us. We need to try to see what is important to others—the parents of our students. Commit to praying for parents daily. As you go down that roll each morning, pray for the parents your students go home to every afternoon.

OTHER EDUCATORS

We've already discussed our relationships with others teachers and staff. Needless to say, they disappoint us as well. The problem with disappointment is that it can paralyze our efforts toward positive relationships if we allow it. Sometimes a team member or coteacher doesn't pull his weight—that disappoints us. Other times a teacher, whom you trusted, betrays a confidence. And sometimes a teacher's behavior toward his or her students dumbfounds and disappoints us. Most often we are disappointed that other teachers don't do or see things the way we do, and we take it as a personal rejection.

I learned early that if you aren't in the room, you may be the one talked about. I felt very out of place at my first school, and my tendency when I feel that way is to isolate myself. I began to eat lunch in my classroom every day under the guise that I had work to catch up on. I never imagined that some of my colleagues thought I was conceited and somehow too good to eat with them. I discovered this one day when I was retrieving my homemade lunch from the refrigerator in the teachers' lunchroom.

"Look who decided to join us," a voice said while my back was turned.

"What have we done to deserve the honor of your presence?" another cackled.

I have to say that it was more difficult for me to even consider eating with these teachers, but it was a wake-up call. I decided not to go back to my room that day. I didn't sit with my critics, but I did stay in the lunchroom. I was disappointed that these teachers, who didn't even know me, had judged me so harshly. But I was also dissatisfied by my avoidance behavior.

How we respond to disappointment is important. If we allow disappointment to turn into hopelessness, we can lose faith. People will disappoint us—sometimes daily. Sometimes we even disappoint ourselves. Do not put your hope in people—or even in yourself. Even those who love us and honor us at times will fail us. We can put our hope in God's unfailing love. Even when all else fails and all others desert you, God will not. Even when life seems to be one disappointment after another, God is good. Even when our trouble is our own fault, God's love never fails.

God gives us instruction about how to deal with those around us, especially if they disappoint us (Rom. 12:12–18). Let's take our focus off of our disappointment and put it on God's unfailing love. There is hope in his love.

- *"Rejoice in hope; be patient in affliction; be persistent in prayer."* We can be joyful when we consider God's unfailing love. Because of the hope we have, we can be patient when things go wrong. And we can be faithful in prayer because we have confidence that God is who he says he is and keeps his promises.
- *"Share with the saints in their needs; pursue hospitality."* We can practice hospitality at school by inviting a colleague to eat with us or spend their planning time with us. We also can bring colleagues something special when we know they are struggling or offer to carry some of their load. Be on the lookout for those in need at your school.
- *"Bless those who persecute you; bless and do not curse."* Slander and gossip are constant visitors to a teachers' lounge. If the words of a colleague sting, find a way to bless the person either in word or deed. But don't do it out of a desperate need for approval—do it out of obedience to the Lord.

- *"Rejoice with those who rejoice; weep with those who weep."*
  Someone else's good news may disappoint you. Maybe you
  didn't get the grant you applied for, but a colleague did.
  Rejoice with your colleague—sincerely. On the other
  hand, someone else's disappointment may be greater than
  your own—comfort her, console her. In both of these ways
  you share the hope of God's unfailing love.
- *"Be in agreement with one another. Do not be proud;
  instead, associate with the humble. Do not be wise in your
  own estimation."* Teachers do not have many opportunities
  for advancement in a school. Sometimes we look to
  increase our own worth by looking down at someone
  else—the substitute, the beginning teacher, the custodian,
  the food service worker, the special education teacher. Do
  not think more highly of yourselves than you ought: "For
  if anyone considers himself to be something when he is
  nothing, he is deceiving himself. But each person should
  examine his own work, and then he will have a reason for
  boasting in himself alone, and not in respect to someone
  else" (Gal. 6:3–4).
- *"Do not repay anyone evil for evil. Try to do what is honorable in everyone's eyes."* We are tempted daily regarding our
  responses to other people. We are all sinners living in a
  fallen world. Therefore, just as someone is bound to disappoint us, we are also bound to respond in anger. This verse
  says we are to do what is right, telling us that we must
  make a conscious decision to do the right thing, think
  before we speak, think before we act.
- *"If possible, on your part, live at peace with everyone."* Even
  when we do everything outlined in this passage, there will

still be people we cannot please and who disappoint us. We can only be accountable for our own actions before God. We therefore should persevere in doing good even when we are utterly disappointed.

According to the National Center for Education Statistics, high levels of staff collegiality are associated with better teacher attendance, more effort, higher morals, and a greater sense of efficacy in the classroom. Disappointment will come, but how we respond to it can determine our perception of job satisfaction. God desires to bless us with satisfaction in our work—it is a gift. But the following key verse of this chapter gives us insight into how we experience that satisfaction. Pray for God's blessing on the work of your hands.

> *There is nothing better for man than to eat,*
> *drink, and to enjoy his work. I have seen that*
> *even this is from God's hand.* **For who can eat and**
> **who can enjoy life apart from Him?**
> ECCLESIASTES 2:24–25
> (EMPHASIS MINE)

Our enjoyment—our job satisfaction—is not dependent upon how others treat us or how others meet our expectations. It is solely dependent upon God and his unfailing love for us. As Solomon, the author of Ecclesiastes said, all else is vanity (Eccles. 1:2 KJV). Don't allow disappointment in yourself or others to distract you from the love of your Heavenly Father. He gave you the gift of teaching and allows you to make a living using the gift he gave you—for his glory! Nothing matters more. Praise and thanksgiving are part of a life of prayer. Can you thank God today for the work he has prepared for you and for which he has perfectly equipped you?

PRAYER POINTS

* *Proverbs 15:13:*
  "A joyful heart makes a face cheerful,
  but a sad heart [produces] a broken spirit."
* *Ecclesiastes 5:12:* "The sleep of the worker is sweet, whether he eats little or much; but the abundance of the rich permits him no sleep."

PRAYER PROMPT

We all experience disappointment as teachers. What is disappointing you now? Lay it at the foot of the cross.

PRAY

Lord, it is so hard for me not to be disappointed that I won't see the fruit of my labor. I realize that my disappointment is of my own making. I realize that I did it all without seeing whose hand it was from. Lord, God, forgive my arrogance! You gave me a job to do, and I need to have joy in the fact that I did the job as well as you prepared me to do. Even Moses did not get to enter the promised land after so many years of struggle and preparation. God showed him the promised land from afar and he was satisfied. Lord, whether or not you show me the promise of the fruits of my labor, let me be satisfied as well. Amen.

Chapter 8

PRAY THE ISSUES

Discouragement

~

Therefore strengthen your tired hands and weakened knees,
and make straight paths for your feet, so that what is lame
may not be dislocated, but healed instead.

HEBREWS 12:12–13

I began to hear the horror stories of burnout even before my first teaching job. As soon as people found out I was going into special education, the "advice" started pouring in. Staying motivated is not an easy task when you are worried about your students' progress day and night. We're encouraged to look for small victories, but a special education teacher sometimes has to settle for minuscule victories.

I had many students whose interpersonal skills were lacking. They didn't know how to get along with others. They either were painfully shy or their behavior was painfully inappropriate. China was an eighth-grade, severely learning disabled girl who basically avoided contact with everyone, including me. I didn't know how to reach her. She was functioning on a third-grade level in reading. I knew that if someone didn't break through her hardened shell, she wouldn't make it through high school. But everything I did just drove her further inside herself.

At some point I stopped trying so hard. After all, she wasn't the only student who needed me. I didn't ignore her, but I no longer went out of my way to engage her. One day toward the end of the school year, there was a gift on my desk. China was absent that day. It was a beautifully crafted beaded change purse. The note attached said, "Thank you for being my teacher." I smiled to myself thinking, *Like I had a choice.* At the end of the day I was told China and her family had moved. My chances to reach her had run out. It really upset me, and I chastised myself for not trying harder.

Looking at the purse, I realized something. This was it—the small victory. China made that purse herself. I still have it to this day. It is a reminder of a seed planted that I pray someone else came along to water after me.

Sometimes just the simplest of steps are enough to encourage us to continue. Sometimes we need to see the "big picture" of God—who he is, where he is, and what his intent is. We all get discouraged, but if discouragement goes unchecked, it can turn into despondency. The circumstances of life can steal our joy. Whether they are physical, emotional, or intellectual, these circumstances can be overcome by the love of God. God has made certain promises to us in time of trouble. Lean on those promises. Claim those promises for yourself in prayer.

WHO IS GOD?

When we are down and discouraged, we turn to ourselves or other people to encourage us. But since the heart is deceitful above all else (Jer. 17:9), we cannot trust our own ability to lift ourselves up. God is the only one who can lift us up. Sometimes we don't turn to God because deep down we don't trust him. We trust in our own abilities more. But God is worthy of our trust. Our dependence need only to lie in him. *Encourage* means "to inspire with courage, confidence, or hope." Who better to encourage then God?

FAITHFUL

> *If we are faithless, He remains faithful,*
> *for He cannot deny Himself.*
> 2 TIMOTHY 2:13

God is faithful, regardless of our previous experiences with man (Rom. 3:3–4).

ABLE

> *And God is able to make every grace overflow to you,*
> *so that in every way, always having everything you need,*
> *you may excel in every good work. As it is written:*
> *He has scattered;*
> *He has given to the poor;*
> *His righteousness endures forever.*
> 2 CORINTHIANS 9:8–9

It is God who equips us to do what we have been called to do. It is God "who is able to do above and beyond all that we ask or think" (Eph. 3:20).

HOLY

> *Lord, who will not fear and glorify Your name?*
> *Because You alone are holy,*
> *because all the nations will come and worship before You,*
> *because Your righteous acts have been revealed.*
> REVELATION 15:4

By his very nature, God is holy. Everything he does is righteous. Everything he does is worthy of praise and worship. And since none of us is righteous—no, not one—we are better off putting our trust in the only one who is.

JUST

> *The Rock—His work is perfect;*
> *all His ways are entirely just.*
> *A faithful God, without prejudice,*
> *He is righteous and true.*
> DEUTERONOMY 32:4

God is a just judge, showing no partiality (1 Pet. 1:17). Everyone who does wrong receives what he should for that wrong. It doesn't matter who we are or what position we hold. It doesn't matter if we are tenured or teacher-of-the-year. Can we say the same? No. Even in the midst of my discouragement, I know that God sees all and gives everyone according to his ways (Jer. 32:19).

Our God is trustworthy. His character demonstrates it. His actions illustrate it. His mercy confirms it. Because he is who he is, I have hope. I am encouraged!

THE INDWELLING

In the midst of a storm we tend to look for God outside of it, asking him to come in and save us. But he is not outside the storms of our lives. He is there right in the middle of them. Even if we are not aware of his presence, he is indeed there. How do we know he is there? His word says so in many places. "And what agreement does God's sanctuary have with idols? For we are the sanctuary of the living God, as God said: 'I will dwell among them and walk among them, and I will be their God, and they will be My people'"

(2 Cor. 6:16). Now we have not received the spirit of the world, but the Spirit who is from God, in order to know what has been freely given to us by God (1 Cor. 2:12). We never walk alone—especially during the most discouraging of times.

GOD IS FOR US

What then are we to say about these things?
If God is for us, who is against us?
ROMANS 8:31

God sent us a helper, a comforter for times of trial and trouble. The Spirit helps us in our weakness and intercedes for us when we pray. Sometimes we are so confused or discouraged that the words to pray don't come. That's when the Spirit, who lives inside of us and knows our every aching, our every desire, prays for us. What an incredible advocate! Jesus himself stands before the Father on our behalf. He took our place, one who knew no sin became sin for our sakes—for *my* sake. God poured out his wrath on Jesus, his only Son, on the cross that day—*for* you, *for* me. He is our champion, our confidante, our defender, our deliverer—our Savior! So when it feels as if no one is on your side or that no one cares about what you care about, remember that the God of the universe is for *you*—you personally.

GOD IS WITH US

"Haven't I commanded you: be strong and courageous? Do not be afraid
or discouraged, for the LORD your God is with you wherever you go."
JOSHUA 1:9

Teachers feel incredibly isolated in their jobs. Even though we are with students all day, we have very little opportunity to build relationships with fellow teachers. So when we are troubled and discouraged, we don't know how to reach out for help. Sometimes we even fear reaching out, thinking it makes us look weak; and in this day and age of accountability, no one wants to appear weak.

Our God *commands* us to be strong and courageous. It's not a suggestion or a piece of practical advice—it's a command! God commands of us things he himself has already equipped us to do. Because he is for us, there is no one worth worrying about who is against us. Even if we are faced with a trial that seems insurmountable, God is with us. He may choose to calm the storm, or he may choose to calm his child. Either way he is there with us. So we have no reason to fear what man might do. God is here, and he's in control!

GOD IS IN US

This is how we know that we remain in Him and He in us:
He has given to us from His Spirit.
1 JOHN 4:13

In the Old Testament, God dwelled among his people in different ways. He accompanied them as a pillar of fire and cloud through the wilderness. He spoke to them through Moses from Mount Sinai. One of the most beautiful expressions of God's love for us is seen in the New Testament. First, he humbled himself and was born as a man to walk among his people. That was a personal, face-to-face relationship. But then he took this very personal relationship one step further. He left his Spirit to reside and abide in the human heart. How much more intimate can a relationship be? He loves us so much that first, he died for us, and second, he placed his Spirit inside those who believe in him so that we could experience his love from the inside out.

HIS PLANS FOR US

Our God is more patient than any of us deserve. Over and over again he is rejected, ridiculed, and refused. Over and over again he forgives, blesses, and accepts us just the way we are. And although we are to fear him—his awesome power demands it—he does not intend us harm but good. Can we see clearly his plans for us?

> *"For I know the plans I have for you"— [this is]*
> *the LORD's declaration— "plans for [your] welfare,*
> *not for disaster, to give you a future and a hope."*
> JEREMIAH 29:11

God spoke of Israel in this verse, but even now his plans for us, the church, are meant for good—his glory. We may find ourselves confused, but God is not the author of confusion, so we can trust in his certainty about what he has in store for us. Sometimes we brace ourselves in fear that God's designs are all against us. But even things that seem to be harmful are for good.

> *We know that all things work together for the good of those who*
> *love God: those who are called according to His purpose.*
> ROMANS 8:28

God's purpose is to bring glory to himself. We are created for such a purpose. God will not give us what we fear or what we selfishly desire. He will give us what he has promised, which is for our best. Knowing this, we are better able to seek him in prayer. When our students don't achieve as we hope or our colleagues treat us with disdain, we can pray that God will be glorified through the situation, that our actions will be representative of a loving God who desires to bless his people.

GAINING ENCOURAGEMENT

Finally brothers, whatever is true, whatever is
honorable, whatever is just, whatever is pure, whatever is lovely,
whatever is commendable—if there is any moral excellence and
if there is any praise—dwell on these things.

PHILIPPIANS 4:8

Schools have reputations. If there is high turnover at a school, that is a red flag and an indicator to many that you wouldn't want to work there. But sometimes you don't have a choice. My first teaching job was a two-hour commute, and I desperately wanted to work closer to home. After two years I finally got my chance. I was so excited about my new prospect and shared my enthusiasm with colleagues where I was teaching at the time. Surprisingly, no one shared in my enthusiasm.

They didn't know anything about my new school, and yet they were finding fault with it. It was in a more prosperous district, and they assumed I would be swimming in a huge budget. It was also a much larger school with more teachers, and they assumed I would get lost in the demands of teachers with more seniority. I started to feel as though they were trying to sabotage my excitement about my new school.

Not everyone was a naysayer, but enough were that it started to bother me. On my last day no one huddled around me to say goodbye and good luck. But one friend walked me out to my car with my last box in her arms. "It's going to be great," she reminded me.

We can choose to listen to the naysayers, or we can focus instead on the good. God directs us to focus on the things above. The world is full of bad reports, so we must consciously focus our prayers on the good and perfect gifts from above instead.

So often we focus on the things that discourage us. Instead we must set our minds on the things above (Col. 3:2), not on the things of the earth. In other words, we must deliberately train our minds to contemplate heavenly things, not earthly ones. This earth and all that is in it is passing away. It is not our reality. It is merely a shadow of what is real—God's will as it is done in heaven.

What specifically should we focus on then? Philippians 4:8 tells us:

- *"whatever is true"*—The Word of God is truth. Time spent studying and memorizing Scripture will help you to focus on the things that are true. Spend a few minutes in God's Word each morning at your desk before your students arrive. It will help set the tone for the rest of the day.

- *"whatever is honorable"*—Our feelings can betray us. The heart is wicked (Jer. 17:9), so it is difficult sometimes to trust our own honesty. Always compare what you say and what you think with what God expects.

- *"whatever is just"*—God is the only just judge. His statutes and judgments fit the behavior of every person without regard for their status in the community. As a teacher, I wanted to be known as a loving, strict, but *fair* teacher. We are tempted every day to be otherwise. Follow God's precepts and you will be a just teacher.

- *"whatever is pure"*—In the world's eyes you may be considered pure. But it's not the world's opinion that matters. We cannot purify ourselves; only God has the power to do that. Ask him to cleanse you completely. Just because everyone else in the teachers' lounge speaks ill of the new principal doesn't make it right. Things are not gray—they are black and white. Pray that God helps you to see the lines clearly and then focus on those things that are pure.

- *"whatever is lovely"*—The world is full of unpleasantness. Our news reports it every day. But we do not have to concentrate on it. We can instead concentrate on those things that are lovely, pleasant, and pleasing. I admit that it is a challenge at the end of a difficult school day, but we can make a deliberate effort to pay attention to those things that are lovely. They will then cause us to pray in thanksgiving to God, the Creator of such things.

- *"whatever is commendable"*—In this age of accountability and the grading of schools, we hear a lot about schools that are failing or being closed. Wouldn't you prefer to hear more about those that are succeeding? Wouldn't you prefer to hear about quality teachers? Find a way within your own sphere to focus on those people and those things that are of good report. Is someone doing something wonderful in your school? Toot her horn! Raise a banner! Strike up the band! Call attention to the good instead of perpetuating the bad reports of others.

OFFERING ENCOURAGEMENT

Blessed be the God and Father of our Lord Jesus Christ,
the Father of mercies and the God of all comfort. He comforts us in all
our affliction, so that we may be able to comfort those who are in any
kind of affliction, through the comfort we ourselves receive from God.
2 CORINTHIANS 1:3–4

I was less than thrilled with my first teaching assignment. It was in a sixth-grade center in an inner-city ghetto. It was frightening to say the least, especially when my own principal told me never to come in early or stay late and never to drive a car there that I cared about. It was two years with absent parents, uncooperative students, no budget to speak of, and chronic classroom vandalism. College did not prepare me for teaching in this environment. But it was that same environment that taught me to be creative in my teaching, my discipline, my communication efforts with parents, and my materials. Because of that experience I've been able to help many others faced with similar situations, and it has been so satisfying to be able to do so.

God comforted me through many trials during my years in the classroom. It was only because I was comforted that I am now able to comfort others. Only teachers really understand what other teachers are going through. Unfortunately, we often keep to ourselves and only communicate our discouragement in the form of a gripe session in the teachers' lounge. Have you been comforted by the Great Comforter? If so, reach out to that brand new teacher and soothe her spirit. Be a listening ear and a praying heart for the veteran who just can't take it anymore. Pray that God will reveal to you who needs to be comforted today. He will show you; just be willing to go where he points.

We have the hope of an eternity with God. Allow that hope to proclaim itself to all those around you. Then when things go wrong and you are at peace, others will want to know how. They will ask you about the hope that is within you. Be ready with your response!

Prayer Points

- *2 Timothy 2:1:* "You, therefore, my child, be strong in the grace that is in Christ Jesus."

- *Hebrews 12:12–13:* "Therefore strengthen your tired hands and weakened knees, and make straight paths for your feet, so that what is lame may not be dislocated, but healed instead."

Prayer Prompt

Often we are discouraged because we try to change things in our own strength. We are unable to do it. Only God can do it through us.

Pray

Lord, it is so difficult to hide my feelings, especially when they border on despair. I want to protect my students from my emotions. I don't want my feelings to get in the way of my teaching and their learning. But when I cover them, I still don't feel at my personal best with the students. Even in this situation I want the peace you have promised—the peace that passes all understanding. Lord, release that peace to me now. Yet if I still experience turmoil, cover any mistakes I might make with your love. Let your love for me trickle down as my love for my students. I will reveal my struggle, and then if I handle it the way you would have me handle it, others will ask about the peace that is within me. Thank you for this time of suffering. Let it work in me patience, perseverance, and finally peace. Amen.

Chapter 9
PRAY THE ISSUES
Danger

~

"Do not show partiality when rendering judgment;
listen to small and great alike. Do not be intimidated by
anyone, for judgment belongs to God. Bring me any case
too difficult for you, and I will hear it."
DEUTERONOMY 1:17

Teachers don't usually love their additional duties at school. Some even avoid them and hope no one notices. When I taught in a middle school, some of our additional duties were hall duty, bus duty, and lunch duty. These were opportunities for us to be visible in hopes of squelching any inappropriate student behavior we might witness outside of class time. I remember seeing my own teachers walk the halls or the bus ramp when I was in school. It always made me feel safe when I saw a teacher, especially as a child who was bullied on more than one occasion throughout her school years.

One of my first experiences with bus duty came when I taught sixth grade. My job was to make sure students were getting on their buses in a timely and safe manner so that everyone could go home. I thought that my very presence would be enough to ensure a smooth transition from the classroom to the bus. I was wrong. I discovered that it took coercion, a little intimidation, and at times physical encouragement. The day I got punched in the face by an unwilling student was the day I realized that I wasn't safe during "duty."

As time went on, we had supervisors from the "Safe Schools" office giving us ways to stay safe at school: Never touch a child, even if it is to break up a fight. Use positive reinforcement to manage students, not negative. And in some schools the advice was even stronger: Don't come in early or stay late. Make sure your classroom is locked at all times. Don't bring anything to school, including a car, you care about. It became increasingly obvious that not only were students not safe at school, but teachers weren't either.

Unfortunately, many teachers had their own unwritten rules about how to stay safe: Keep your door closed, especially when you hear a commotion in the hallway. Don't get involved. Look the other way if you see trouble starting during duty. Such responses aren't right, but they certainly are understandable.

Everyone agrees that schools are not as safe as they used to be. Teachers don't feel safe. Students don't always feel safe. Parents pull their children home to school them during the junior high and high school years for this very reason. Contrary to media reports, God has not been "kicked" out of the public schools. No one can "kick" God out of anywhere. He is there, in the thick of it. He was with you when the fight broke out in the hallway. He was with you when a student brought a gun to school. He was with you when you came in early and found your classroom vandalized. God has promised to be with you—through it all. Pray daily for his protection and preservation over you and your students. Be willing to run under the shelter of his wings.

GOD PROTECTS US, NOT FENCES AND METAL DETECTORS

Do not fear, for I am with you;
do not be afraid, for I am your God.
I will strengthen you; I will help you;
I will hold on to you with My righteous right hand.
ISAIAH 41:10

The Psalms are filled with David's fear of the enemy surrounding him and seeking his life. He went immediately to God each time. Even though he had soldiers of his own, even though he himself was prepared to defend or fight, David knew his only real protection came from God. Some schools use metal detectors to ensure that no weapons end up on campus. Others employ security officers to patrol the hallways. Teachers are advised not to get in the middle of student fights. They are instructed, informally, not to worry about what goes on just off school property even if it's a matter of three feet. We are encouraged to do whatever it takes to protect ourselves since the school isn't really equipped to protect us.

But God wants us to know that he is completely capable of protecting us. That doesn't mean that we sit there and do nothing. It does mean that we know that God is in complete control, and whatever happens can eventually bring him glory. I'm sure the students at Columbine High School could never have predicted the impact the life and death of Cassie Bernall had not only on the teachers and students, but also on the rest of the country. God was indeed glorified.

GOD PROTECTS THE OPPRESSED

The LORD is a refuge for the oppressed,
a refuge in times of trouble.
PSALM 9:9

School can be an oppressive place for teachers and students. I can vividly remember what it was like to walk the hallways in my junior high and high schools. I didn't quite fit into any group. I had very few friends. For the most part, I was invisible—until someone with a cruel sense of humor would notice me just for the purpose of humiliating me. In all my years in public school, there was only one teacher who made me feel as bad as those bullying boys (and girls). Only one. Most of my other teachers invited me into a relationship with them and offered me a place of refuge. Pleasing those teachers became my goal. It made the peer challenges manageable.

God is waiting with open arms to shelter the oppressed. I wish I had known that when I was a teenager. We can know it for ourselves as teachers—teachers who don't fit the mold, teachers whose world-view doesn't resemble that of their colleagues, teachers who spend their lunch breaks alone in their rooms. God is there for you. Take shelter under his wings.

> *Be gracious to me, God, be gracious to me,*
> *for I take refuge in You.*
> *I will seek refuge in the shadow of Your wings*
> *until danger passes.*
>
> PSALM 57:1

GOD PROTECTS US EVEN WHEN WE FALL

> *Though he falls, he will not be overwhelmed,*
> *because the LORD holds his hand.*
>
> PSALM 37:24

I have fallen into sin periodically as a teacher in the classroom. I found myself falling into the sin of pride more often than not. Humility isn't preached to new teachers. We are encouraged instead to rely on our expertise and place of power in a school. Pride is supposed to be a confidence builder since many of us feel so uncertain when we first enter the classroom.

But I wasn't a beginning teacher the day I fell. I had returned to work after being home for five years with my two sons. I couldn't find a teaching assignment, so I took a job offered to me at the district office as an assistant to a supervisor. It was to me a step up from teaching. I was taking classes toward my master's degree in Educational Leadership at the time, and to me this was an opportunity to perfect my leadership skills.

I wanted to prove myself more valuable than some lowly assistant. So when my supervisor gave me my first assignment, I was quite confident I could execute it expertly. I had to track down a missing camcorder reported stolen from a local high school. This would be easy since the assistant principal at that high school was a former colleague of mine.

When I began to question John about his handling of the robbery, I didn't receive the cooperation or respect I thought I would. John thought I was accusing him of ineptness and went on the attack. It was really my own incompetence that was on display. John filed a complaint about me to my supervisor. I was demoted to desk work the very next day.

The bottom line in this story is that I was prideful and arrogant. The combination of those two sins led to disaster. I rashly rushed into a role I thought had inherent power and respect. I had to be reminded that power and respect are earned, not bestowed. Yet at the same time, even though I fell, God upheld me with his hand. I received earthly consequence for my sin, but the Father protected me from complete ruin. It gave me an opportunity to respond to my punishment the way God wanted me to, thereby giving glory to God.

At times we find ourselves in difficult, and sometimes dangerous, situations as a result of our own sin. If you find yourself in that place, it will sorely hurt, but you are not abandoned. Pray for forgiveness and for God's protection.

GOD PROTECTS US FROM EVIL

But the Lord is faithful; He will strengthen and
guard you from the evil one.
2 THESSALONIANS 3:3

Satan, the evil one, is not happy that you belong to the Living God. In fact, he will do whatever it takes to tarnish you so that your actions tarnish God's reputation. But our God is faithful. He will set us on firm ground with his precepts and statutes. If we stand firm on this ground, we will be protected. If we choose to walk outside and away from this firm foundation, we will find ourselves in quicksand and outside of God's protection. We must be on our guard!

Be sober! Be on the alert!
Your adversary the Devil is prowling around like a roaring lion,
looking for anyone he can devour.
1 PETER 5:8

A HIDING PLACE

[S]o that through two unchangeable things, in which it is
impossible for God to lie, we who have fled for refuge might have
strong encouragement to seize the hope set before us.
HEBREWS 6:18

In Corrie ten Boom's book *The Hiding Place*, we learn through her experiences in the horrors of Nazi Germany that there is no pit so deep that God's love is not deeper still. "Corrie herself said, 'Every experience God gives us, every person he puts in our lives, is the perfect preparation for the future only he can see.' Corrie's Christlikeness in the face of terrifying circumstances has prepared untold readers to face their own futures with faith in God's ultimate triumph over evil."[1]

Even when things seem at their worst, remember that you are experiencing only as much as God permits. And what he permits, he does so for our perfecting. But until that time of our perfection, we can hide under the shelter of his wings. Christ already bore the storm himself, so that we might be sheltered from its deadly intensity.

What Is Our Response?

It is encouraging to find out that God is our refuge and strength in times of danger and trouble. We can rest in that fact and cast all of our anxieties on him. But we do have a responsibility to seek his refuge and his peace, as well as lead others to that same safe place. But in order to be a refuge for others, we must first find it for ourselves.

Seek His Refuge

Over and over again in the Scriptures *refuge* is mentioned as something that man takes. It is a deliberate choice—for the righteous man who seeks God's ways. In the Psalms, David continually sought God's refuge. He knew that was the only safe place when he was surrounded and attacked by his enemies more than once. In the books of Samuel we see the same pattern. David knew from whom his redemption came and offered songs of praise and thanksgiving as his response. We can all remember times when God saved us from our enemies and sometimes saved us even from ourselves. Remarkable preservations should be particularly mentioned in our praises. Be careful not to look to your own abilities to save yourself from a particular consequence or attack. As teachers we experience condemnation, wrongful accusations, and attacks almost daily. Run to God. Seek his refuge first and foremost.

SEEK PEACE

When a man's ways please the LORD,
He makes even his enemies to be at peace with him.
PROVERBS 16:7

When I taught in the projects of Tampa, Florida, I was confronted many times with those who sought to do me harm. Some of them were only four feet tall and twelve years old! One particular boy was the smallest sixth grader I've ever met, but his anger was bigger than any adult. He came to my care in anger, but I was determined that he wouldn't leave it in anger. This child did everything in his power to create havoc in my life as his teacher. He rejected any and all attempts to be "at peace" with me. It didn't matter that I wasn't the cause of his anger—I just happened to be the one in the way of it at this time in his life. I wasn't in fear of him until one Monday morning when I entered my "locked" classroom after an extended weekend. The room was trashed to say the least. The brand new computers I gained for our classroom from a grant I wrote were turned over on the floor. All of my supplies were deliberately strewed all over the room. The windows were broken. And horror upon horrors, there was human feces atop my teacher's desk. I wouldn't have known who had done such horrible things against me except that he left a note on the blackboard for all to see.

How could I possibly bring peace to this relationship, especially if this student didn't want peace? God says, "If possible, on your part, live at peace with everyone" (Rom. 12:18). To me that meant I had to do everything in my power to live at peace with this child. He was still punished by the principal, but after his ten-day suspension, I knew I had to find a way.

First, I had to see him as God sees him—a child in need of a Savior. But as a public school teacher I was limited in what I could and could not say to him about his Savior. So it was up to me to exemplify Christ's love for him—even when all I really wanted to do was wash my hands of him altogether. Second, I decided to bless him at every turn—positive reinforcement! It didn't always help, but I stayed consistent, and he began to trust me. If he was in need, I was right there to meet that need. If he was discouraged, I tried to encourage him. When I noticed he had a hidden talent for music, I complimented him on it.

By the end of the year, there was peace, not love and total acceptance but peace nonetheless. I never got an apology for the "incident," nor did I require one. I never saw this child again, but I know that during our time together a seed was planted. If someone hasn't already, perhaps someday someone else will come along in his life and water that seed and bring it to harvest.

Seek the ways of God first and then seek peace. Both are required for others to see the Lord. You may be just the one to show them.

> *Pursue peace with everyone, and holiness—*
> *without it no one will see the Lord.*
>
> HEBREWS 12:14

BE A REFUGE FOR YOUR STUDENTS

Do you remember being afraid to raise your hand in class? I do. Even when I taught in the classroom, it was a struggle to get kids to feel safe enough to raise their hands. It put them in a vulnerable position—not just with me but with their peers. No one wants to look stupid, so for many kids it's better not to be noticed at all.

I admit that some kids seem to have a "Pick Me" sign on their foreheads and whose hands are always up. But if you give in to their constant appeal for attention, you take the risk of alienating those children who really need your attention. It's a matter of balance. Calling on students regardless of whether their hands are raised is fine as long as you've already created a safe environment in which the wrong answer isn't ridiculed and there's not always one right answer.

We need to strive to engage all of our students as often as possible. Class participation is very important. If participation is not a common occurrence in your class, then you should honestly assess whether or not you run a safe classroom. Encourage children to question and teach them to think. Our God expects the same from us. And he's made the foot of his throne a safe place to bring those questions and concerns. Ask the Lord to reveal to you anything you're doing that hinders his children from coming to him. After all, if they can't come to you with their questions and you belong to the Father, how will they know it's ever safe to go to him?

Children need to feel safe if they are to be successful learners. You may remember a time in your life when you didn't feel safe in a classroom. Maybe you were humiliated by a teacher for not being smart enough. Maybe a teacher was so intimidating that you were fearful whenever you were in his or her class. No matter how we feel as adults in our schools, we are, in fact, adults—our students are not. They deserve teachers who make their classroom a nonthreatening, safe place to be. Even if they have to walk through metal detectors to get to your room, make sure that when they arrive they breathe a sigh of relief!

PRAYER POINTS

- *Ezekiel 3:9:* "'I have made your forehead like a diamond, harder than flint. Don't be afraid of them or discouraged by [the look on] their faces, even though they are a rebellious house.'"
- *1 Corinthians 16:13:* "Be alert, stand firm in the faith, be brave and strong."
- *2 Timothy 1:7:* "For God has not given us a spirit of fearfulness, but one of power, love, and sound judgment."

PRAYER PROMPT

Schools are not as safe as they used to be. Can you at least make your classroom a safe place for all students? Pray that God will create a haven in your classroom.

PRAY

Heavenly Father, school is so different than it was when I was in school. Teaching is so different from what I expected it to be as a teacher. Some days I feel as if I am just waiting for the straw that will break this camel's back. Finding myself in danger is a pretty big straw! Yet you have promised to preserve me when I come in and when I go out each day. Build a hedge of protection around me, Lord. Protect me from those who seek to hurt me. And then show me what I must do to be an encouragement to them as well. You have said that we must love our enemies and pray for those who persecute us. I pray for the ones now who desire to harm me. Draw them to yourself. Make known your love for them. Amen.

Chapter 10

PRAY THE ISSUES
Lack of Respect

~

Honor everyone. Love the brotherhood.
Fear God. Honor the Emperor.
1 PETER 2:17

I graduated college when I was twenty-one years old. I looked seventeen. Imagine my dismay upon my student teaching assignment—high school seniors who had been left behind one or more times. Many of them were nineteen-year-old boys, football players, and bigger than I was! It was bad enough that other teachers had mistaken me for a student, but I saw the look on these students' faces on the first day of school. They believed they had it made—I was no threat.

I knew it was important that I stake my territory as their authority figure right away. But how? They talked when I talked. They did all sorts of things when my back was turned to write on the board. And one boy in particular would ask to go to the rest room and never come back. I was in trouble, and it was only the first week of school.

High school students are like sharks. They can smell fear. My anxiety turned to fear one day when an oversized fullback towered over me to tell me he'd sit down when he was good and ready to sit down and not a moment before. The weekend came, and I was desperate to find a way to get these students to listen to me. What would happen during my first teacher evaluation? Disaster loomed.

I remembered vividly what it felt like to be in high school. I prayed that somehow I could use that to my advantage. That Monday I came to school prepared. Anton, my chronic bathroom privilege abuser, asked again if he could go to the rest room. I told him no because I couldn't trust him not to skip out. Standing there at my desk with his back to the class, Anton puffed up, looking bigger than his six-feet-two-inches, two hundred pounds. "You can't stop me if I have to go," he seethed.

"I wouldn't dream of it," I said and then held up a Styrofoam cup. "If you've really got to go, I have an alternative."

Can you imagine? Anton took the cup from my hand and threw it in the garbage. He returned to his seat and never again asked me if he could go to the rest room. I didn't humiliate him. No one in the class heard our exchange. I just offered him another option. Anton never really liked me, but he didn't cross me either. Eventually, the rest of the class followed his lead. I was grateful that I could still speak the language of a high school student without dishonoring God. I prayed for clarity of mind and for the Spirit to guide my tongue and choose my words. God gave me what I needed when I needed it.

In a Schools and Staffing Survey by the U.S. Department of Education, 89 percent of teachers said that student disrespect of teachers is a problem in school; 79 percent say verbal abuse of teachers by students is a problem. Most teachers agree that they are not satisfied with the esteem of society for the teaching profession. Statistics aside, teachers are discouraged. Lack of respect for their position is probably one of the greatest discouragers they face.

Another common complaint is that they are not treated as professionals by other school personnel or by society at large. In this chapter I want to challenge you to think about who you are and what you do differently from what you have done for at least the past fifteen years. Teaching is not in fact a profession. Teaching is a calling.

We are not drawn to teaching for the prestige or the salary. Nor are we enticed into it with signing bonuses or the promise of the excitement of being on the cutting edge. Most people become teachers because they already possess the gift of teaching and desire to impact the lives of children—they want to make a difference. That is not a definition of a *profession* but of a *vocational calling.*

We therefore have no promise of respect, status, or unrivaled influence. But we are still discouraged and disappointed by the lack of respect for teachers. How can we embrace our calling and at the same time detach from our expectations of high regard and high esteem? The key is focus. We must focus our thoughts and energies on the work God has called us to do. We must stop looking in the mirror and start looking at the cross. Even Jesus wasn't welcomed by his own people. Even in his hometown his authority was not recognized. "And they were offended by Him. But Jesus said to them, 'A prophet is not without honor except in his hometown and in his household'" (Matt. 13:57). We can overcome the lack of respect that exists in and for schools and teachers today by first giving respect ourselves to those to whom it is due. Start by praying for them. It will change your heart toward them if you have difficulty finding kind words for them.

RESPECT FOR ELDERS

"You are to rise in the presence of the elderly and honor the old.
Fear your God; I am the LORD."
LEVITICUS 19:32

It still amazes me that I was so arrogant as a beginning teacher. I felt so prepared, so equipped to do what I felt called to do. I'm a person who is into the details of life, and so when I planned for my first day of teaching in an elementary school, I was sure I had everything covered. I taught gifted students—each grade on a different day. Mondays were for kindergarten and first grade, Tuesdays were for second grade, and so on. My students traveled by bus from their regular school once a week to spend the day with me at a school they didn't know. It was new for me, and it was new for them. But I had it all under control—or so I thought.

With wide eyes my little ones entered the room and surveyed their new surroundings. It was perfectly decorated in an organized yet creative fashion. I encouraged them to look for their names so they could find their seats. I just assumed that as highly gifted students they all could read their names. Billy Sanders wandered from desk to desk and station to station. He began to get more and more agitated. Unfortunately, I didn't notice Billy's confusion until he was a tearful mess in the middle of the floor. If you know anything about five-year-olds, you know crying can be contagious. Some of the other students began to cry because it was obvious to them that there must be something to cry about. Before I knew it, the class had exploded into a chorus of crying.

The commotion caught the attention of my neighboring teachers, and they hurried into my room to the rescue. Together they redirected the children and had them all sit in a circle on the floor, their eyes now dry, waiting for me to begin their day. I sat down in their midst and gave a telling look of thanks to my colleagues. Before they left, one teacher squeezed my shoulder and said, "I'm here if you need anything." I can't tell you how grateful I was. Before that moment of chaos, I didn't even know, nor would I ever admit, that I needed any help. God did equip me, but he did it with others he provided to come to my aid.

Maybe you're a beginning teacher. Maybe you're a veteran with thirty years of experience. Either way, there usually will be someone else at your school who is older or more experienced than you are. That person who is older or wiser can be a treasure to you. That person has inside information about how your school works and how children learn. Aside from the practical, that person deserves your respect according to God.

If you are a new teacher, don't be afraid to ask questions or glean from the wisdom of seasoned teachers. Look to the experience of others who have gone before you. They are there to offer comfort as well as guidance. Commit to praying for each member of your faculty, but pay special attention to those who came before you. They may be exactly what God intended to meet your need.

I know you may not always feel as if those who are older or more experienced are there to support you. Teachers tend to be territorial in nature. We also tend to feel isolated from our colleagues. Take the first step to get to know your colleagues. Visit their classrooms at the end of the day to say hello. Compliment them on something they did with their students. Sit with them at lunch. You will find that you have more in common than just the place you work. Look for ways to honor them as often as you can.

RESPECT FOR THOSE IN AUTHORITY

Don't brag about yourself before the king,
and don't stand in the place of the great.
PROVERBS 25:6

Teachers who have been teaching for a long time or teachers who have transferred to a new school are especially at risk for this prideful behavior. Our principals and administrators are appointed authorities over us as teachers. When a new principal comes to a school, often many of the teachers already at that school put in for transfers. Some teachers on the road to becoming principals "exalt" themselves in front of the existing principal. These are not honoring behaviors. They are born out of dishonoring attitudes.

We need to allow the king to be the king. We need to step aside in humility when another is in charge—even if the king is difficult to follow, to say the least. Not all educators will be as happy to be in education as you are. And there will be times when you will not see eye to eye, but stay focused on your true mission. The only way to have peace in the midst of adversity is to silently choose not to harbor any ill feelings, overlook any trespasses, and move on. When entering a new school, get to know your leadership and operate within those parameters.

As long as your principal or administrator doesn't ask you to sin, you are obliged to obey and honor him or her. It may be the most difficult thing you've ever had to do. God will bless you when you put your own pride aside and let the king be the king. It ultimately brings him the glory. Pray for those in authority. They will be expected to give account one day about how they treated those in their charge. They need our prayers to hold them up in the middle of the incredible odds against them.

RESPECT FOR THE HOST

"But when you are invited, go and recline in the lowest place,
so that when the one who invited you comes, he will say to you,
'Friend, move up higher.' You will then be honored in the
presence of all the other guests."
LUKE 14:10

When I came back to the classroom after five years at home with my children, I thought I could just pick up where I left off. I had gained a place of honor at my old school and was well respected by my principal and colleagues. I was a leader. I made the mistake upon reentering teaching that I could reclaim my previous status. But this was a new school for me, and to my new principal and colleagues, I was still a beginner.

Here are some of the things I didn't know: I didn't know the temperament of my principal, I didn't know who the gatekeeper was at our school (was it the secretary or the teacher workroom aide or the cafeteria manager?), I didn't know which teachers supported the principal and which didn't, and I didn't know whether the special education teacher was an equally valued member of the entire faculty. There were many more things I didn't know, like where to park in the parking lot and where not to, but I learned those as I went along. Unfortunately, I discovered that what was true at my old school was completely the opposite at this school. After many mistakes, I backed off from my assumption that I knew what I was doing and from volunteering for leadership roles. I deferred to taking a backseat as a part of this faculty and let those who came before keep their seats. It took two years before either my department head or my principal asked me to take any additional responsibilities at our humble school. When they did, I knew it was because they believed I knew what I was doing too.

Even though it is a principal's job to get to know his teachers, it is just as crucial for a new teacher to take time to get to know the culture of his school. What is valued? What are the rules? Who has the power? Being watchful, learning, and working within the parameters of your school's environment help ensure your ability to make changes and adjustments later, when it really counts. Learn your school's culture; adapt and become part of the mold before you try to break it.

Your new school is your *host,* at least until you become an integral part of it and later become the host yourself. Take the lesser place voluntarily. Don't force your way in. If that means parking out in the grass when others have a place of honor, park there. Do it with humility and grace, and the host will bring you to the head of the banquet table someday. Pray that God will reveal to you any sinful pride and cultivate a meek and mild spirit in you instead.

RESPECT FOR ONE ANOTHER
Show family affection to one another with brotherly love.
Outdo one another in showing honor.
ROMANS 12:10

This verse speaks specifically to believers about believers. God was always gracious to me when I worked in a public school. He revealed to me other teachers who were believers. I was also so grateful not to be alone. Even when my children started school and I volunteered at their school, God revealed the workroom aide as a Christian along with several teachers. I caught them praying in a closet one morning. I discovered this was a daily routine, to pray in that closet, and I asked if I could join them. What a wonderful blessing it is to work with *one another!*

Sometimes, however, knowing that a teacher at your school is a fellow believer becomes a stumbling block. Sometimes we take one another for granted. Other times we find fault more quickly because we hold them to a higher standard than other teachers or staff. And sometimes we ignore them altogether, believing they are just fine on their own. We are called to regard one another with a preference and desire to spend time with one another over time spent with others. This doesn't mean we can't be a positive influence on the other teachers and staff at our schools, but it does mean we should delight in being with one another.

When things go wrong—and they will—to whom will you turn for support, guidance, and encouragement? Go to another Christian teacher. Advice from nonbelievers may be right according to the world's view, but it may not be right according to God. We daily are faced with situations and emotions that tie us in knots inside and confuse us. Who else but another believer can help you navigate the murky waters safely? God put you together in this place for one another and so that your fellowship might glorify him. It is a precious treasure, set aside just for you to find. Don't waste it!

Do nothing out of rivalry or conceit,
but in humility consider others as more important than yourselves.
PHILIPPIANS 2:3

Teachers rarely receive recognition for their accomplishments in the classroom. We end up looking for recognition anywhere we can find it, even on the most trivial level. During a monthly technology committee meeting, one teacher boasts about how her personal contact is what made the school networking possible. "It's who you know!" she announces. During a faculty meeting the principal announces that Miss Shimler, the science teacher, has offered to take on extra duties without compensation. Miss Shimler puffs up in her chair and graciously accepts her principal's praise. During the annual district Teacher-of-the-Year nominations, Mr. Radcliff submits his own name and convinces many of his colleagues to do so. "I'll have to make it happen myself. The system is rigged!" he defends. None of these scenarios speaks highly of the teacher involved.

I know that often teaching is a thankless job, but God encourages us to be patient in affliction and to persevere. Instead, look for opportunities to esteem a colleague above you. Is there a teacher whose humble demeanor makes her accomplishments with children invisible? Is there a new teacher who you heard would love to sponsor the drama club this year, but you've done it for the past ten? Step down and offer her your place. When you are looking for ways to esteem others, you take the focus off of yourself—and that's exactly what God wants you to do. True humbleness of heart will not go unrecognized. Wait for others to praise you instead.

PRAYER POINTS

- *Luke 14:10:* "But when you are invited, go and recline in the lowest place, so that when the one who invited you comes, he will say to you, 'Friend, move up higher.' You will then be honored in the presence of all the other guests."
- *Philippians 2:3:* "Do nothing out of rivalry or conceit, but in humility consider others as more important than yourselves."

PRAYER PROMPT

Are some student's disrespectful words still ringing in your ears? Commit to pray for this student daily and ask God to love him through you.

PRAY

Lord, although I traditionally receive gifts from my students during the holidays, this year it came when I needed it the most. There are so many times when I wonder if what I do matters. The gifts show appreciation, but when a parent goes out of her way to write me a note of thanks, I am moved. Even though I am grateful for the outpouring of appreciation, I must remember that it is not the yardstick used to measure success. Help me to be mindful of what really matters, Lord. Help me to focus on the eternal rewards and not the temporal ones. You caution us not to build up our treasures here on earth because it will all pass away eventually. And if we focus on earthly treasure, we won't be focused at all on the heavenly ones. Keep me focused, Lord. Amen.

Chapter 11
PRAY THE ISSUES
Lack of Funds

*The one who loves money is never satisfied with money,
and whoever loves wealth [is] never [satisfied] with income.
This too is futile. When good things increase, the ones who
consume them multiply; what, then, is the profit to the owner,
except to gaze at them with his eyes?*

ECCLESIASTES 5:10–11

My first two years of teaching were in an inner-city school in Tampa, Florida. I taught in special education and had little or no budget. I was given one hundred dollars for the school year. That was to cover the cost of copy paper, art supplies, office supplies, and curriculum. As a first-year teacher I had no idea what to expect. This was not covered in my teacher prep program at the university. As a beginning teacher in the district I participated in a Beginning Teacher Program and attended monthly meetings and monthly "make-and-takes." We were encouraged to do the best with what we had and to make the rest. I spent many hours on the floor surrounded by magazines that I cut apart for a variety of classroom and curriculum needs. I learned how to make do. Two years later I transferred to a closer district that was much more prosperous. My yearly budget skyrocketed! To me I had struck gold. But the other teachers who had taught in this district for some time were always disappointed. I couldn't understand it—I was just plain grateful.

The adage *the more money you have, the more money you spend* is true even for teachers and schools. To say that money is the answer to all of our problems is both shortsighted and misleading. What do we say then to the rural or inner-city or Native American reservation educator who reaches her students and leads them to succeed? According to research, money is not a motivator to attract or retain teachers. Teachers are teaching because they love children and want to make a difference. Teachers have been successfully changing the lives of students for generations with very little funding. Somehow we've equated the offering or provision of money with our value as teachers. It just isn't so.

On the other end of the spectrum are teachers close to retirement. With these teachers there is a great deal of "calculation" going on in order to decide if they can even afford to retire. Unfortunately, in some districts teachers are discovering that the money they put into their retirement systems has shrunk for one reason or another and is not going to be adequate. In order to balance budgets some districts choose solutions that put retirement monies at risk. How can teachers respond in a way that pleases God when faced with such a challenge to their financial well-being? We need to counsel one another according to biblical principles so that we don't sin in either our anger or our disappointment. The enemy knows we are vulnerable when it comes to our finances. He will use that weakness to get us to curse God. Pray that in your weakness God will be strong. Pray that your actions and reactions bring glory to him. Pray that your responses will make others wonder about the hope that is within you.

GOD GIVES MONEY, NOT THE STATE

The LORD brings poverty and gives wealth;
He humbles and He exalts.

1 SAMUEL 2:7

We are conditioned to believe that our provision comes from men. We worry about whether the current bond issue will pass. We criticize our state's decisions about public school funding. In a private school we worry about enrollment and tuition. These are all real-life matters, but God is in control. He is our provision. Any and all funding we have comes from him. The news is full of articles about low teacher salaries, budget cuts, and arguments over whether the property taxes should be raised to better fund education. Admittedly, our country shows what it values by how it spends its money. But God is the one who makes a man rich and makes a man poor, all for the glory of his name.

It may not seem fair, but if we know the source of our provision, then we can rest in it. Worrying about it will not make the money come any faster. God provides us with ways to increase our gain, whether through grants or incentives or even tobacco money. He can soften the hearts of the people to pass a bond issue or raise property taxes if he chooses to—but he is not obligated to. Sometimes what feels like a famine is really God perfecting his people. God does and will continue to provide.

I used to worry that if I didn't fill in the gaps with my own money, my students would go without. I didn't want them to experience need. I wanted to be able to meet every need and every desire. Sometimes my own self-serving actions delayed God's blessing because I tried to "fix" the budget problems myself.

It wasn't just the school's budget shortfall that worried me. It was our family budget. My husband cringed every time we entered an office supply store. He knew we'd come out with much more than we intended that day. "Isn't there a central supply closet at your school?" he'd ask. I'd just roll my eyes at his ignorance. All teachers know that when you run out of things, you're out. So we buy what we can when we can.

Unfortunately, spending our own money can hinder the cause of teachers more than it helps. The budget crunch is not felt by key decision makers when teachers spend their own money trying to fix the problem themselves.

Try to remember, when tempted to supplement your classroom from your own funds, that your generosity may be masking budget insufficiencies that desperately need to be revealed. Although it can be very inconvenient and frustrating, going through the wait or a little red tape reveals the need, so things can change. Sometimes it's better to do without in order to highlight a problem within. Another reason we shouldn't rely on our own ability to "fix things" is that we become self-reliant instead of God-reliant. We can lay all this at the throne of grace in prayer, even that last ream of copy paper in our closets when it's only February!

Focus first on being the best teacher you can be for your students. Use the gift God has given you to meet the needs of his children. Let God take care of the money.

GREAT PROVISION CAN MAKE US FORGET GOD

"And your herds and flocks grow large, and your silver and gold multiply, and everything else you have increases, [be careful] that your heart doesn't become proud and you forget the LORD your God who brought you out of the land of Egypt, out of the place of slavery."

DEUTERONOMY 8:13–14

Sometimes all that glitters is so distracting that we can forget God, the one who saved us and brought us out of our own wilderness. There is much said about the arrogance of the rich man in the Bible. But everyday we are tempted to forget God. When I transferred from a poor district to a rich district, I was thrilled. I finally had a decent budget and didn't have to scrounge around for materials for my students. I could relax! And I did relax. I became so comfortable that I began to focus on what all this money could do for my students and the prestige of any additional money I brought in through grants. I forgot my original focus, which was what God could do for my students through me.

We only seem to remember God when things go wrong. Everyone claims that our character is built through the tough times, but my pastor recently said that it is during the easy times, the times of plenty, that our character is truly tested. Can we maintain our focus on God when all is well? That is the greater challenge. Consider your current school budget situation. Are you experiencing a time of plenty? Be on guard that you don't forget God. Make sure the praise goes to him. Make sure you look for opportunities to share your abundance with others.

GREAT RICHES CAN PROMOTE SELF-SUFFICIENCY

A rich man is wise in his own eyes,
but a poor man who has discernment sees through him.
PROVERBS 28:11

We rely on our own abilities and gifts especially when our budgets are large and stable. We think it is our own doing that things are going so well, especially when others are struggling. The last district I taught in prided itself on its thriftiness in times of plenty so that in times of hardship they would still have an abundance. Their behavior in money matters did not seem unlike that of Joseph while in Egypt. Although I doubt it was the result of a prophetic word from God or a vision. It was men and women making sound financial decisions. You'd think we would have been grateful that in times of severe budget cuts our district's programs and teacher salaries remained steady—but we weren't. We were greedy for more. Just enough was not good enough. We whined and complained about the low salary increases and rejected program proposals. We mistakenly believed that it was our own doing that protected us from hardship and became ungrateful for what we had.

God appoints our leaders, and if we are to be rich school districts, he has provided for that. If we are to be a poor district, he has provided for that as well. If you live and work in a poor district and you understand from whom your provision comes, seek him out. Be grateful for your dependence. If instead you live and work in a rich district, be careful not to misunderstand from whom your provision comes and deny him.

> *Anyone trusting in his riches will fall,*
> *but the righteous will flourish like foliage.*
> PROVERBS 11:28

PRAISE GOD FOR YOUR ABUNDANCE

> *"Riches and honor come from You,*
> *and You are the ruler of everything.*
> *In Your hand are power and might,*
> *and it is in Your hand to make great and to give strength to all."*
> 1 CHRONICLES 29:12

God is the Great Provider. Everything we have belongs to him. We are called to be good stewards of however much he has given us. What seems an abundance to me may not seem an abundance to you. But we are encouraged to be faithful with a little before we will have the opportunity to be faithful with much. There are several points to remember concerning abundance:

- Remember to ascribe your abundance to God (1 Chron. 29:12).
- Do not put your trust in your abundance, but in God alone (Job 31:24).
- Do not boast in your abundance (Deut. 8:17).
- Do not hoard your abundance (Matt. 6:19).

To whom much is given, much is expected. Be mindful of this. Look for ways to use your abundance to show God's love to others. Let your generosity be your trademark, and when they ask, "Why do you give it away?" you can say, "Because God provided it for that very purpose."

DO NOT BE HIGH-MINDED

Instruct those who are rich in the present age not to be arrogant or to set their hope on the uncertainty of wealth, but on God, who richly provides us with all things to enjoy.

1 TIMOTHY 6:17

A high-minded person is someone who is arrogant. Arrogance is particularly hated by God. Isaiah 5:21 says, "Woe to those who are wise in their own opinion and clever in their own sight." We've been taught that pride goes before a fall. It is easy to be prideful when you work in a brand-new, technology-leading school, where every teacher has her own office and telephone. But this abundance isn't the work of your own hands. And even if it were, it is God's gift to you. False humility is just as woeful to God. So when you are at a districtwide meeting and someone asks you at which school you teach, don't shyly say its name, knowing it will conjure up images of prestige and plenty.

False humility is seen just as often when we are in need. I, myself, must be careful when I talk about my first years of teaching in an inner-city school and how we had nothing. Yes, I learned how to be creative. Yes, I learned to make something out of nothing. Yes, I learned how to be content with very little. But if I boast about those things, I am prideful—even though in the world's eyes I have the right to boast of my strong character. But it's not the world's opinion of me that I worry about—it's God's. What's his opinion of your response to your budget situation?

Our value is not determined by any dollar amount. Our value is in Christ alone. We are forgiven because he was forsaken. We are accepted because he was condemned. We are able to enter the throne room of the Most High God with full confidence because Christ proclaims us worthy. We are sons and daughters of the King, sharing in the inheritance with Jesus.

The Spirit Himself testifies together with our spirit that we are
God's children, and if children, also heirs—heirs of God and
co-heirs with Christ—seeing that we suffer with Him so that
we may also be glorified with Him.

ROMANS 8:16–17

PRAYER POINTS

- *Luke 3:14:* "Some soldiers also questioned him: 'What should we do?' He said to them, 'Don't take money from anyone by force or false accusation; be satisfied with your wages.'"

- *Mark 4:19:* "'But the worries of this age, the seduction of wealth, and the desires for other things enter in and choke the word, and it becomes unfruitful.'"

PRAYER PROMPT

Are you struggling with contentment with your budget situation? Pray for contentment and seek God's forgiveness if you have placed too much importance on money.

PRAY

Lord, everyone around me is deceived. They believe that the root problems in education are related to lack of money. I cannot change the minds of those who disperse funds. I can only go to the one who disperses wisdom. You are the answer to all of education's problems. I will be accountable to you for how I spend my money. We need a change of hearts, not a change in policy. Search my heart, Lord, and reveal any selfish motives. Change my heart, Lord, and let that change others. Amen.

Chapter 12

Prayer in Schools and out of Schools

"Again, I assure you: If two of you on earth agree about any matter that you pray for, it will be done for you by My Father in heaven."

MATTHEW 18:19

My first experience of prayer in school was when I was in high school. During eleventh grade I stumbled upon a morning prayer meeting in an Algebra teacher's classroom. It was called the Logos Club. I actually saw a poster advertising this early morning gathering and decided to investigate. I couldn't find an empty seat in that crowded classroom. Students spilled out into the hallway with their necks craning toward the sound of uplifted prayer from within. I remember being amazed—amazed that such a thing had been going on at our school for years without my knowing it. The Logos Club became my refuge. I felt as though God provided it just for me. It was a haven. It was a place I went as many mornings as I could to help me focus myself for the day. God showed me that year that I wasn't alone and that he was right there in the thick of it with me.

From then on I craved an opportunity to teach in a school where everyone prayed, where everyone believed. During my internship I chose a private Christian school for my semester placement. The teachers did pray together every morning before the students arrived, but somehow it seemed forced and hollow. The principal led them but in a way that I sensed was not genuine. I was disappointed. The atmosphere of the school seemed more oppressive than any public school I had ever been a part of. I transferred to another school midterm.

PRAYER IN SCHOOL

Our oldest son, Christopher, attends a public middle school. He also participates in an AWANA youth club at our church. His participation in that club requires him to memorize Bible verses every week. He was having difficulty finding time to do this memory work, so I suggested that he take his handbook to school and memorize during his study hall. He was very reluctant. After numerous conversations, he finally confided that he didn't think he was allowed to bring his Bible verse book to school. He assumed that since he was in a public school, the Bible was against the rules. I then educated our son about what the law says and that he was perfectly permitted to read his Bible while at school.

Prayer in school occurs on many different fronts. Teachers pray on their own at their desks. Teachers pray in groups before or after school hours. Students pray on their own at their desks. Students pray in groups before or after school hours. Parents pray with students and teachers in groups on school grounds on special occasions. Parents also pray with teachers and students on campus before or after school hours. Prayer is going on all the time in our schools. Maybe you're like my son—not sure what is really allowed—or afraid of the resistance that may indeed come if you pray or read your Bible at school. Be encouraged. The law supports you, and Christian teachers everywhere are praying to support your desire to pray God's word at school.

What the Law Says

Praying in school is not against the law. In fact, the U.S. Constitution guarantees students the right to pray in public schools. It is a protected form of free speech. A student can pray on the school bus, in the hallways, in the cafeteria, in their student-run Bible club, at the flagpole, in the sports stadium, and elsewhere on school grounds. They can even pray silently before and after class in the classroom. Teachers have these same rights and may pray in their classrooms silently, in the hallways, in the teachers' lounge, in their teacher-run prayer time before or after school.

The problem comes when a teacher or student wants to pray as an organized part of the school schedule a prayer specific to a particular religion. This book, however, promotes individual silent prayer on the part of teachers and group prayer before or after school. We are not called to public prayer in order to "show off."

> *"Whenever you pray, you must not be like the hypocrites, because they love to pray standing in the synagogues and on the street corners to be seen by people. I assure you: They've got their reward! But when you pray, go into your private room, shut your door, and pray to your Father who is in secret. And your Father who sees in secret will reward you."*
> MATTHEW 6:5–6

Consider the motives of your heart when you decide to pray in school. Ask God to first reveal your motives to make sure they are pure. Pray because the Spirit has led you to pray. Pray because your heart breaks for your students, parents, and colleagues. Pray for God's will to be done on earth as it is already in heaven. Never pray to be heard or to make a statement.

RESISTANCE TO PRAYER IN SCHOOL

As you know, schools are keenly aware of anything that might be construed as either discriminatory, unconstitutional, or open to a lawsuit. Some administrators are not educated about what the law really says about prayer in school and may be resistant to your efforts to begin a prayer group on campus. If your principal is a believer, he or she still may have reservations.

Resistance can also come from parents. Some parents may feel that a Christian prayer group violates the church and state rulings. It does not. There are actively anti-Christian parents in our schools. One teacher who leads a student prayer and Bible time before school said that when he attended "See You at the Pole" at his school outside last year, a parent called to complain that district employees should not be paid from public funds if they are involved in religious activities during their normal work day. This teacher decided that the way around this was to pray before the workday begins.

High schools may experience resistance from another front. A local high school prayer group meets off campus because Wiccan and homosexual groups also demanded the right to meet on campus. Administration consequently banned one as opposed to having them all.

God says we should expect resistance. How we handle that resistance is what really counts. "I believe that a polite, but firm, response to any resistance would be the best approach. One could explain that the meetings are within the law, conducted on private time, and approved by the principal. In some cases, it might be appropriate to invite resistors to attend and observe the group in action," shares a middle school teacher who leads a teacher prayer group on campus.

The enemy will not be happy that you are leading students or teachers to pray. He will look for ways to discredit you, discourage you, and dare you to continue. When resistance rears its ugly head, remember

- not to be surprised
- Jesus has already overcome the world
- you are on the right path
- you are within your rights
- to handle it with grace
- to pray for God's protection
- that the reasons to pray heavily outweigh the resistance not to pray

ENCOURAGEMENT TO PRAYER IN SCHOOL

We are called to encourage one another. If you have the gift of encouragement, minister to other believers in your school. More and more groups are supporting teachers who pray in and for their schools. Your own church should be an encouragement to you to pray together as a group. Parents who pray and let you know that they pray for you are also an encouragement. Just the fact that prayer is your best defense against the enemy should encourage you to pray.

As teachers come together to pray, they develop a deeper relationship with one another than they would otherwise. School can feel like a place of isolation to many teachers. There is very little time to build collegiality. When teachers choose to meet before or after school to pray together, the walls come down, and they find themselves united in purpose. Whether you are the assistant principal, the special education teacher, the gym teacher, or the language arts department head, you are on equal footing before God. Together you can make your requests known to him.

TEACHER PRAYER GROUPS

The greatest benefit of our group to me as a teacher is the support of Christian brothers and sisters in my workplace. I know that I can bring any need, work-related or not, and the group will listen and pray with me. Because we have an active Moms in Touch group at our school, with a representative who attends our prayer meetings, I know that our concerns will also be lifted up by this supportive parent group.

Middle school math teacher
Colorado Springs, Colorado

Earlier in this book I told the story of a time when I stumbled into the prayer time of a group of teachers at my children's elementary school. As a parent, just knowing that these teachers were committed to prayer in and for their school made my heart glad.

Christian Educators Association International (www. ceai.org) works to support Christian teachers, especially those working in public schools. Their resources for teacher prayer are wonderful. In an article called "Public Schools Need Power Prayers" on the CEAI Web site, author and speaker Judy Turpen offers teachers and parents five types of prayers to empower Christian educators in public schools. If you decide to form a group of your own, these prayers will help you focus your energies.

1. *Jericho Prayers*—Enlist the support of two or three others and begin to walk around your school once a week. Pray for the teachers, the administration, the support staff, parents, and teachers. Pray for teachers to teach in love, for administrators to provide an atmosphere of religious freedom, for

support staff to assist those they're assigned to work with, for parents to take an interest in their children's studies, and for students to have a safe educational environment, a campus where learning can take place.

2. *Nehemiah Prayers*—Christian educators need those who will fast and pray as the people of God did in Nehemiah 9. Teachers can do this themselves if need be. In Nehemiah's day the people stood and confessed the sins and iniquities of their fathers. They stood and read the Word of God, and they worshiped the Lord their God. Fasting is not a secret formula to twist God's arm or a legalistic prayer ritual. Fasting is a desperate cry of the heart and an act of humility and repentance. "When fasting is accompanied by grief over sin and repentance from sin, it leads to new resolve and compensating action; it can be both useful and therapeutic. When it becomes an end in itself, it is sterile and counterproductive" (John Watts).

3. *Aaron and Hur Prayers*—Teachers get weary fighting the battles of modern education. Often they are called upon to spend time dealing with unruly children, impatient principals, government paperwork, and a host of other items unrelated to what they were called to do: teach! Joy would fill the heart of any teacher if she knew two or three members of her church were praying for her on a regular basis. Just as Aaron and Hur held up Moses' arms, commit to hold up the arms of a teacher in your congregation. Even as believing teachers in the same school, you can pray for each other on a regular basis.

4. *Habakkuk Prayers*—Habakkuk 3 reminds us of God's awesome power, his creative ability, his glory throughout the

earth, and the reverential fear of who he is. Educators can empathize with the closing verses of the chapter:

> Though the fig tree does not bud
> and there is no fruit on the vines,
> though the olive crop fails
> and the fields produce no food,
> though there are no sheep in the pen
> and no cattle in the stalls,
> yet I will triumph in the LORD;
> I will rejoice in the God of my salvation!
> Yahweh my Lord is my strength;
> He makes my feet like those of a deer
> and enables me to walk on mountain heights!
>   (vv. 17–19)

Teachers need to know this is their powerful God. We can pray for public schools when we drive to work. Instead of "drive-by shootings" we can institute "drive-by prayers."

5. *Esther Prayers*—Called Christian teachers are placed in the classroom for just such a time. God sets up rulers and kings, and I believe he also places the "right" teachers in the "right" classroom. When difficult situations arise, such as confronting a student, an administrator, or a parent, teachers need those who will gather and pray in order to put a shield of faith around them. Teachers are empowered when they know they have the power of prayer with them in their daily tasks.[1]

Prayer in school is not only allowable, but it is necessary. First, we need to break the cycle of isolation as teachers. We need to come together as brothers and sisters in Christ and face head-on with prayer what troubles us, what discourages us, and even what frightens us. We can pray on our own, but prayer that is shared is powerful indeed.

PRAYER OUT OF SCHOOL

In some situations prayer on campus does not seem possible. Of course, you can always pray silently wherever you are at school, but organized group prayer among teachers may not happen. You can still work in a prayed-for school! There are ways for every boy and girl to be prayed for by name. There are ways for every building to be prayed for on a daily basis. There are ways for churches in the community to pray. The first step is to make your prayer requests known to those outside the school. Consider excerpts from the article "Prayer Warriors" by Denise Amos.[2]

> Have you ever wondered what it would be like to have each of your students bathed in prayer every day? What could God do in a class or school where students and faculty were prayed for by name every morning? Well, Jan Butler, my daughter's fifth grade teacher, not only imagined it, but she set up a plan to make it a reality. Each of her fifth grade students has a prayer warrior.
>
> Jan asks every member of her Home Bible Fellowship and Sunday school class at her church to commit to praying for one of her students every day. Jan and these supporters of Christian teachers in public schools believe Ephesians 3:20: "Now to him who is able to do immeasurably more than all we ask or imagine, according to his power that is at work within us, to him be glory." Each prayer partner receives a child's name and prays for this child to come to know and love Jesus. Jan asks them to

pray that the children will show kindness and cooperation with fellow students. They also ask that God help these children to quickly learn new facts and recall previous knowledge.

Wow! Don't you wish you had thought to do this for your students? Don't you wish someone else was praying for your child every day?

Not only are children's lives being touched through Jan's prayer warriors, but Jan's mother prays for Jan every day and Jan's husband, Pat, prays for her principal every day. Jan has asked and imagined great things for her students and I believe the whole school can tell that something immeasurable is happening with Jan Butler's students.

Most of Jan's students did not have the opportunity to meet or hear about their prayer buddy, but the prayers supported Mrs. Butler and her students during the entire year. Who knows, maybe a lifetime!

MOMS IN TOUCH

Moms in Touch International is an organization that encourages two or more moms to meet for one hour each week to pray for their children, their schools, their teachers, and their administrators. Included are mothers, grandmothers, or anyone who is willing to pray for a specific child and school. These are moms who believe that prayer makes a difference. The purposes of MIT include:

1. To stand in the gap for our children through prayer.
2. To pray that our children will receive Jesus as Lord and Savior, then stand boldly in their faith.
3. To pray for teachers and staff.

4. To pray that teachers, administrative staff, and students would come to faith in Jesus Christ.
5. To provide support and encouragement to moms who carry heavy burdens for their children.
6. To pray that our schools may be directed by biblical values and high moral standards.
7. To be an encouragement and a positive support to our schools.[3]

CHURCH PRAYER

Our churches are perfect places to pray for teachers, students, and parents. We want to pray for each group so that they will be open and interested in the gospel. Youth groups within the church can also play a powerful role.

PRAYER WALKS

In her best-selling book, *Prayer Walk*,[4] Janet Holm McHenry shows what it takes to pray for a school. Janet teaches high school English, journalism, and creative writing, AND she prayer walks around her school on a regular basis. Walk around your school either during your lunch break (although it's usually too short!) or before/after school and lift the names of students, teachers, administrators, and parents in prayer.

PRAYER ONLINE

Teachers and prayer are no strangers to the virtual world. The CEAI Web site and my own Web site, EncourageTeachers.com, both offer teachers message boards to post their prayer requests. If you can't seem to break the isolation you feel in your school, look online for ways to connect with other teachers who are willing to pray with and for you.

CREATING YOUR OWN TEACHERS-IN-PRAYER GROUP

One teacher involved in a teacher prayer group at her school shares this. "I have tried doing the job of teaching without the support of a prayer group at school. The job is hard work, which can border on impossible at times, and prayer support at school can make an enormous difference. My experience is that it will be worth whatever effort it takes to get a group going. If you are aware of other staff members who are believers, you might be able to start by inviting them to join you for prayer, and then pray for God to bring opportunities for you to encourage others to come alongside. Our group started up this time with just two people, and it has grown considerably since then. If you don't know of other believers, 'See You at the Pole' on the third Wednesday of September is a good opportunity to get in touch with other believers on the staff and among students and parents. It is nice to have parents attend the group to bring a different perspective and also to lend prayer support to the group. As a word of caution, if parents are present, it is necessary to be discreet about mentioning names of staff and students when praying for specific situations to protect privacy. It would also be a courtesy to inform the principal of your plans and seek approval."

Teachers in prayer is not a new phenomenon, but we live in such a time that we can no longer afford to keep our faith to ourselves. Our schools are in need of renewal and revival. Prayer calls that revival into being. The only way to break the cycle of teacher isolation is to enter into community. Haven't we been alone in this long enough? It's time to stand on the Word of God and commit to prayer—together. I'll leave you with the end of a poem by Phil Migliorati, Mission America, adopted by CEAI and included for your consideration. Look at it as a call to arms—arms joined in prayer!

I'll pray for my school. You pray for yours!
I'll pray for my students. You pray for yours!

I'll pray for my fellow teachers, administrators, and school employees. You pray for yours.

I'll ask those I serve, school and city officials, fellow teachers, administrators, students, and parents to pray for our school. You ask those you serve to do the same.

I'll join a teachers prayer group at school and if there is none, I'll begin one even if it is only two gathering for prayer before or after school. You do the same.

I'll ask my pastor and church to pray for our school. You ask your pastor and church to pray for your school.

I'll encourage the youth ministry at our church to get involved in my school. You do the same.

Prayer Points

- *Luke 22:32:* "'But I have prayed for you that your faith may not fail. And you, when you have turned back, strengthen your brothers.'"
- *Romans 1:12:* "That is, to be mutually encouraged by each other's faith, both yours and mine."
- *Galatians 6:2:* "Carry one another's burdens; in this way you will fulfill the law of Christ."

Prayer Prompt

Are you currently part of a teacher prayer group? Pray daily for your members. If not, then ask the Holy Spirit to lead you with regard to starting a group.

PRAY

Heavenly Father, I know that you call us to pray together in your name. I also know that the enemy will be roused to prevent us from doing so. Help me to be courageous in the face of resistance and even outright hostility, remembering that it is you they reject. Encourage me and nourish me daily through your Word so that I might know how to answer everyone. Pour your grace upon me as I step out in faith to meet with other believing teachers to pray for our students, their parents, and our colleagues. Let it be so that when others see us, they finally know who you are and it is a sweet aroma to them. Amen.